easy to make!
Favourite
Family Meals

Good Housekeeping

easy to make!
Favourite
Family Meals

COLLINS & BROWN

First published in Great Britain in 2008
by Collins & Brown
10 Southcombe Street
London W14 0RA

An imprint of Anova Books Company Ltd.

The Good Housekeeping website is
www.allaboutyou.com/goodhousekeeping

10 9 8 7 6 5 4

ISBN 978-1-84340-439-2

A catalogue record for this book is available from the British
Library.

Reproduction by Dot Gradations Ltd
Printed and bound by Times Offset (M) Sdn. Bhd, Malaysia

Keep updated. Email food@anovabooks.com for FREE email alerts
on forthcoming titles.

This book can be ordered direct from the publisher. Contact the
marketing department, but try your bookshop first.

www.anovabooks.com

NOTES

- Both metric and imperial measures are given for the recipes. Follow either set of measures, not a mixture of both, as they are not interchangeable.
- All spoon measures are level.
  1 tsp = 5ml spoon; 1 tbsp = 15ml spoon.
- Ovens and grills must be preheated to the specified temperature.
- Use sea salt and freshly ground black pepper unless otherwise suggested.
- Fresh herbs should be used unless dried herbs are specified in a recipe.
- Medium eggs should be used except where otherwise specified. Free-range eggs are recommended.
- Note that certain recipes, including mayonnaise, lemon curd and some cold desserts, contain raw or lightly cooked eggs. The young, elderly, pregnant women and anyone with an immune-deficiency disease should avoid these, because of the slight risk of salmonella.
- Calorie, fat and carbohydrate counts per serving are provided for the recipes.
- If you are following a gluten- or dairy-free diet, check the labels on all pre-packaged food goods.
- Recipe serving suggestions do not take gluten- or dairy-free diets into account.

Picture Credits
Photographers: Nicki Dowey (pages 33, 34, 35, 36, 37, 41, 42, 43, 50, 52, 54, 55, 57, 58, 59, 69, 71, 72, 74, 76, 77, 78, 82, 85, 88, 91, 92, 93, 94, 102, 103, 104, 110, 111, 112, 113, 115, 116, 117, 118, 119, 120, 122, 123, 125 and 126); Craig Robertson (all Basics photography plus pages 32, 38, 40, 44, 45, 47, 53, 60, 62, 63, 65, 68, 75, 80, 81, 83, 89, 95, 99, 100, 101, 106 and 107);
Lucinda Symons (page 96)
Stylist: Helen Trent
Home Economist: Alice Hart

Contents

Foreword

Getting supper on the table every evening for the family is the real challenge for most cooks. Not only is time usually short because there's so much else going on, trying to think of something different to cook night after night can be a trial.

I really believe that cooking midweek meals can be just as quick and easy as heating up a ready-meal, and twice as rewarding. Making the effort is well worth it. Sitting down to eat together not only gives the family a chance to talk about their days but also means you know exactly what's in the food you're eating.

To inspire you we've put together a collection of speedy meals that take minutes to put together, storecupboard suppers for nights when there's no time to shop and more elaborate recipes for when you've got longer in the kitchen, as well as indulgent puddings for when the family deserves a treat.

The book includes 101 ways to feed your family well, every day. All the recipes have been triple tested in the Good Housekeeping kitchens to make sure they work every time.

Emma

Emma Marsden
Cookery Editor
Good Housekeeping

0

The Basics

2 **3**

Separating

You'll need to separate eggs for making sauces such as mayonnaise, soufflés, meringues, and some cakes. It's easy, but it requires care. If you're separating more than one egg, break each one into an individual cup. Separating them individually means that if you break one yolk, you won't spoil the whole batch. Keeping the whites yolk-free is particularly important for techniques such as whisking.

1 Crack the egg more carefully than usual: right in the middle to make a break between the two halves that is just wide enough to get your thumbnail into.

2 Holding the egg over a bowl with the large end pointing down, carefully lift off the small half. Some of the white will drip and slide into the bowl while the yolk sits in the large end of the shell.

3 Carefully slide the yolk into the smaller end, then back into the large end to allow the remaining white to drop into the bowl. Take care not to break the yolk; even a speck can stop the whites from whisking up.

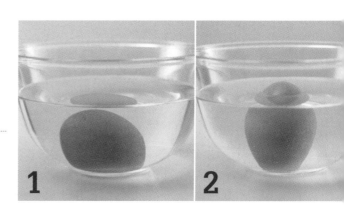

1

Preparing eggs

There are only three essentials to basic egg preparation: cracking, separating and whisking – and once you have mastered these simple techniques you will be able to cook eggs in lots of different ways.

How can I tell if my eggs are fresh?

A fresh egg should feel heavy in your hand and will sink to the bottom of the bowl or float on its side when put into water (1).
Older eggs, over two weeks old, will float vertically (2).

Whisking

1 Use an electric or hand whisk. Make sure that there is no trace of yolk in the whites and that the whisk and bowl are clean and dry. At a low speed, use the whisk in a small area of the whites until it starts to become foamy.

2 Increase the speed and work the whisk through the whites until glossy and soft rounded peaks form. Do not over-whisk as the foam will become dry and grainy.

Making pancakes

To make eight pancakes, you will need:
125g (4oz) plain flour, a pinch of salt, 1 medium egg, 300ml (½ pint) milk, oil and butter to fry.

1 Sift the flour and salt into a bowl, make a well in the middle and whisk in the egg. Work in the milk, then leave to stand for 20 minutes.

2 Heat a pan and coat lightly with fat. Coat thinly with batter.

3 Cook for 1½ –2 minutes until golden, carefully turning once.

2

3

4

Preparing vegetables

These frequently used vegetables can be quickly prepared to add flavour to savoury dishes: onions and shallots have a pungent taste that becomes milder when they are cooked, and are often used as a basic flavouring, while tomatoes and peppers add depth and richness to a variety of dishes. Garlic and chillies are stronger flavouring ingredients.

Onions

1 Cut off the tip and base of the onion. Peel away all the layers of papery skin and any discoloured layers underneath.

2 Put the onion root end down on the chopping board, then, using a sharp knife, cut the onion in half from tip to base.

3 **Slicing** Put one half on the board with the cut surface facing down and slice across the onion.

4 **Chopping** Slice the halved onions from the root end to the top at regular intervals. Next, make 2–3 horizontal slices through the onion, then slice vertically across the width.

Shallots

1 Cut off the tip and trim off the ends of the root. Peel off the skin and any discoloured layers beneath.

2 Holding the shallot with the root end down, use a small, sharp knife to make deep parallel slices almost down to the base while keeping the slices attached to it.

3 **Slicing** Turn the shallot on its side and cut off slices from the base.

4 **Dicing** Make deep parallel slices at right angles to the first slices. Turn it on its side and cut off the slices from the base. You should now have fine dice, but chop any larger pieces individually.

Peeling tomatoes

1 Fill a bowl or pan with boiling water. Using a slotted spoon, add the tomato for 15–30 seconds, then remove to a chopping board.

2 Use a small sharp knife to cut out the core in a single cone-shaped piece. Discard the core.

3 Peel off the skin; it should come away easily depending on ripeness.

Seeding unpeeled tomatoes

1 Halve the tomato through the core. Use a small sharp knife or a spoon to remove the seeds and juice. Shake off the excess liquid.

2 Chop the tomato as required for your recipe and place in a colander for a minute or two, to drain off any excess liquid.

Seeding peppers

1 Cut the pepper in half vertically and snap out the white pithy core and seeds. Trim away the rest of the white membrane with a knife.

2 Alternatively, cut off the top of the pepper then cut away and discard the seeds and white pith.

Cook's Tip

The seeds and white pith of peppers taste bitter so should be removed before you use the peppers. Some people find pepper skins hard to digest. To peel raw peppers, use a swivel-handled peeler to cut off strips down the length of the pepper. Use a small knife to cut out any parts of skin that the peeler could not reach. Alternatively, chargrilling whole peppers gives them a smoky flavour and makes them easier to peel.

Chargrilling peppers

1 Hold the pepper, using tongs, over the gas flame on your hob (or under a preheated grill) until the skin blackens, turning until black all over.

2 Put in a bowl, cover and leave to cool (the steam will help to loosen the skin). Peel.

Garlic

1 Put the clove on a chopping board and place the flat side of a large knife on top of it. Press down firmly on the flat of the blade to crush the clove and break the papery skin.

2 Cut off the base of the clove and slip the garlic out of its skin.

3 **Slicing** Using a rocking motion with the knife tip on the board, slice the garlic as thinly as you need.

4 **Shredding and chopping** Holding the slices together, shred them across the slices. Chop the shreds if you need chopped garlic.

5 **Crushing** After step 2, either use a garlic press or crush with a knife: roughly chop the peeled cloves and put them on the board with a pinch of salt. Press down hard with the edge of a large knife tip (with the blade facing away from you), then drag the blade along the garlic while still pressing hard. Continue to do this, dragging the knife tip over the garlic to make a purée.

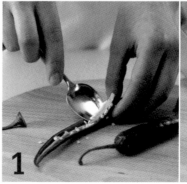

Chillies

1 Cut off the cap and slit open lengthways. Using a spoon, scrape out the seeds and the pith.

2 For diced chilli, cut into thin shreds lengthways, then cut crossways.

Cook's Tip

Wash hands thoroughly after handling chillies – the volatile oils will sting if you accidentally touch your eyes.

Preparing fruit

A few simple techniques can make preparing both familiar and not-so-familiar fruits quick and easy.

Segmenting citrus fruits

1 Cut off a slice at both ends of the fruit, then cut off the peel, just inside the white pith.

2 Hold the fruit over a bowl to catch the juice and cut between the segments just inside the membrane to release the flesh. Continue until all the segments are removed. Squeeze the juice from the membrane into the bowl and use as required.

Preparing mangoes

1 Cut a slice to one side of the stone in the centre. Repeat on the other side.

2 Cut parallel lines into the flesh of one slice, almost to the skin. Cut another set of lines to cut the flesh into squares.

3 Press on the skin side to turn the fruit inside out, so that the flesh is thrust outwards. Cut off the chunks as close as possible to the skin. Repeat with the other half.

Preparing papaya

1 If using in a salad, peel the fruit using a swivel-headed vegetable peeler, then gently cut in half using a sharp knife. Remove the seeds using a teaspoon and slice the flesh, or cut into cubes.

2 If serving on its own, halve the fruit lengthways using a sharp knife, and use a teaspoon to scoop out the shiny black seeds and fibres inside the cavity.

Zesting citrus fruits

1 Wash and thoroughly dry the fruit. Using a vegetable peeler, cut away the zest (the coloured outer layer of skin), taking care to leave behind all the bitter white pith. Remove as much zest as you need.

2 Stack the slices of zest on a board and, using a sharp knife, shred or dice as required.

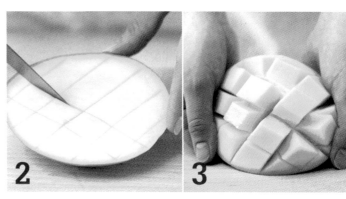

Cooking pasta, rice and potatoes

The popular staples of pasta, rice and potatoes transform meat, poultry, fish and vegetable dishes into substantial meals. Perfectly cooked rice and pasta are super-quick accompaniments, while potatoes are one of the most versatile of all vegetables.

Cooking pasta

There are a number of mistaken ideas about cooking pasta, such as adding oil to the water, rinsing the pasta after cooking and adding salt only at a certain point. The basics couldn't be simpler. Rinse the pasta after cooking only if you are going to cool it for serving as salad, then drain well and toss with oil. Filled pasta is the only type of pasta that needs oil in the cooking water – the oil reduces friction, which could tear the wrappers and allow the filling to come out. Use 1 tbsp for a large pan of water.

Dried pasta

1 Heat the water with about 1 tsp salt per 100g (3½ oz) of pasta. Bring to a rolling boil, then put in all the pasta and stir well for 30 seconds, to keep the pasta from sticking.

2 Once the water is boiling again, set the timer for 2 minutes less than the cooking time on the pack and cook uncovered.

3 Check the pasta when the timer goes off, then every 60 seconds until it is cooked al dente: tender with a bite at the centre.

4 Drain the pasta in a colander. Toss with your chosen sauce.

Fresh pasta

Fresh pasta is cooked in the same way as dried, but for a shorter time.

1 Bring the water to the boil.

2 Add the pasta to the boiling water all at once and stir well. Set the timer for 2 minutes and keep testing every 30 seconds until the pasta is cooked al dente: tender but with a little bite at the centre.

Basmati rice

Put the rice in a bowl and cover with cold water. Stir until this becomes cloudy, then drain and repeat until the water is clear. Soak the rice for 30 minutes then drain before cooking.

Long-grain rice

1 Use 50–75g (2–3oz) raw rice per person; measured by volume 50–75ml (2–2½fl oz). Measure the rice by volume and put it in a pan with a pinch of salt and twice the volume of boiling water (or stock).

2 Bring to the boil. Turn the heat down to low and set the timer for the time stated on the pack. The rice should be al dente: tender with a bite at the centre.

3 When the rice is cooked, fluff up the grains with a fork.

Cooking rice

There are two main types of rice: long-grain and short-grain. Long-grain rice is generally served as an accompaniment, while short-grain rice is used for dishes such as risotto, sushi and paella. Long-grain rice needs no special preparation, although basmati should be washed to remove excess starch.

Basic risotto

Italian risotto is made with medium-grain arborio, vialone nano or carnaroli rice, which release starch to give a rich, creamy texture. It is traditionally cooked on the hob, but can also be cooked in the oven.

To serve four, you will need:
1 onion, chopped, 50g (2oz) butter, 900ml (1½ pints) hot chicken stock, 225g (8oz) risotto rice, 50g (2oz) freshly grated Parmesan, plus extra to serve.

1 Gently fry the onion in the butter for 10–15 minutes until it is very lightly coloured. Heat the stock in a pan and keep at a simmer. Add the rice to the butter and stir for 1–2 minutes until well coated.

2 Add a ladleful of stock and stir constantly until absorbed. Add the remaining stock a ladleful at a time, stirring, until the rice is al dente (tender but still with bite at the centre), about 20–30 minutes. Note: you may not need all the stock.

3 Stir in the grated Parmesan and serve immediately, with extra cheese passed separately.

Boiling potatoes

1 Peel or scrub old potatoes, scrape or scrub new potatoes. Cut large potatoes into even-sized chunks and put them in a pan with plenty of salted cold water.

2 Cover, bring to the boil, then reduce the heat and simmer until cooked – about 10 minutes for new potatoes, 15–20 minutes for old.

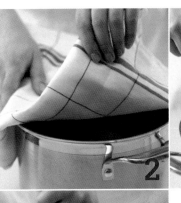

Mashing potatoes

For four people, you will need:
900g (2lb) floury potatoes such as Maris Piper, 125ml (4fl oz) full-fat milk, 25g (1oz) butter, salt and ground black pepper.

1 Peel the potatoes and cut into even-sized chunks. Boil as above until just tender, 15–20 minutes. Test with a small knife. Drain well.

2 Put the potatoes back in the pan and cover with a clean teatowel for 5 minutes, or warm them over a very low heat until the moisture has evaporated.

3 Pour the milk into a small pan and bring to the boil. Pour on to the potatoes with the butter and season.

4 Mash the potatoes until smooth.

Roasting potatoes

To serve eight to ten, you will need:
1.8kg (4lb) potatoes, peeled and cut into large chunks, 3 tbsp vegetable oil, 75g (3oz) unsalted butter, 6 rosemary sprigs, 6 garlic cloves, salt and ground black pepper.

1 Preheat the oven to 200°C (180°C fan oven) mark 6. Put the potatoes in a pan of salted water, cover, bring to the boil, and simmer for 5–6 minutes. Drain and return to the pan over a low heat. Shake until the potatoes are dry and a little fluffy.

2 Heat the oil and butter in a roasting tin. Put the potatoes in the tin with the rosemary and garlic. Toss to coat evenly in oil and butter, and season. Cook for 1 hour, turning from time to time until the potatoes are brown and crisp. Adjust the seasoning and serve.

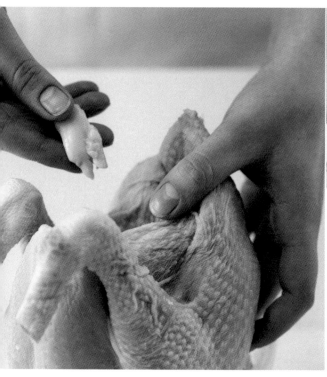

Cleaning

Before stuffing a chicken or other bird for roasting, clean it thoroughly. Put the bird in the sink and pull out any loose fat with your fingers. Run cold water through the cavity and dry the bird well using kitchen paper.

Hygiene

Raw poultry and meat contain harmful bacteria that can spread easily to anything they touch.
Always wash your hands, kitchen surfaces, chopping boards, knives and equipment before and after handling poultry or meat.
Don't let raw poultry or meat touch other foods.
Always cover raw poultry and meat, and store in the bottom of the refrigerator, where it can't touch or drip on to other foods.

Preparing poultry

One of the most versatile meats, poultry – and especially chicken – makes wonderful hearty dishes. It's economical to buy a whole bird and joint it rather than buying joints and it is quite quick and easy to do yourself.

Jointing

1 Using a sharp meat knife with a curved blade, cut out the wishbone and remove the wings in a single piece. Remove the wing tips.

2 With the tail pointing towards you and the breast side up, pull one leg away and cut through the skin between the leg and breast. Pull the leg down until you crack the joint between the thigh bone and ribcage.

3 Cut through that joint, then cut through the remaining leg meat. Repeat on the other side.

(continued)

4 To remove the breast without any bone, make a cut along the length of the breastbone. Gently teasing the flesh away from the ribs with the knife, work the blade down between the flesh and ribs of one breast and cut it off neatly. (Always cut in, towards the bone.) Repeat on the other side.

5 To remove the breast with the bone in, make a cut along the full length of the breastbone. Using poultry shears, cut through the breastbone, then cut through the ribcage following the outline of the breast meat. Repeat on the other side. Trim off any flaps of skin or fat.

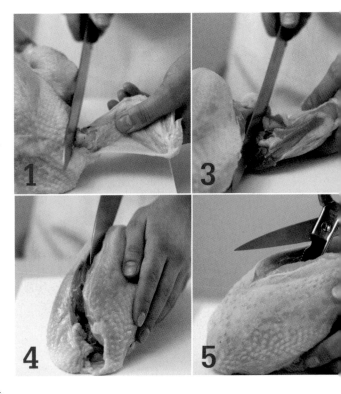

Simple roast chicken

To serve four to six, you will need:
1.4kg–1.6kg (3–3½ lb) chicken, 5 garlic cloves, 4 lemon slices, juice of 2 lemons (keep the squeezed halves), 2 tsp Dijon mustard, 4 sprigs each of fresh rosemary and thyme, 1 sliced onion, 300ml (½ pint) chicken stock, 300ml (½ pint) dry white wine.

1 Make small incisions all over the chicken except for the breast. Loosen the breast skin. Crush 3 garlic cloves and slip under the skin with the lemon slices, mustard and herbs.

2 Put the lemon halves inside the cavity. Put the chicken in a roasting tin. Spoon 2 tbsp lemon juice into the cavity and pour the remaining juice over. Chill for a few hours. Take out of the refrigerator 30 minutes before cooking.

3 Preheat the oven to 200°C (180°C fan oven) mark 6. Put the chicken, breast down, on a rack in the tin. Add the onion, remaining garlic and 4 tbsp each of the stock and wine. Roast for 20 minutes, then turn and roast for 35–40 minutes or until the juices run clear when the leg is pierced. Baste occasionally, adding wine if needed.

4 Put the chicken on a serving dish and cover with foil. Spoon off the fat, leaving the juices in the tin. Put the tin over a medium-high heat, add the remaining stock and wine and stir, scraping the sediment from the tin. Simmer for 5 minutes to make gravy. Strain.

Roasting and carving chicken

A roast chicken has a luxurious aroma and flavour, and it makes an excellent Sunday lunch or special meal with very little preparation. To get the most out of the roast these few simple guidelines make carving easy, giving neat slices to serve.

Roasting times

Roast for 20 minutes per 450g (1lb) plus 20 minutes at 200°C (180°C fan oven) mark 6.

How to check your chicken is cooked

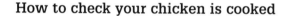

Test by piercing the thickest part of the meat: the juices should run clear.

Carving

1 Starting at the neck end, make slices about 5mm (1/4 in) thick.

2 To cut off the legs, cut the skin between the thigh and breast. Pull the leg down to expose the joint with the ribcage. Cut through that joint. (For small birds, cut through the joint between thigh and drumstick.)

3 To carve meat from the leg (turkeys and very large chickens), remove leg from the carcass as above. Joint the two parts of the leg. Holding the drumstick by the thin end, stand it up on your carving board and carve slices parallel with the bone. Carve the thigh flat on the board or upright.

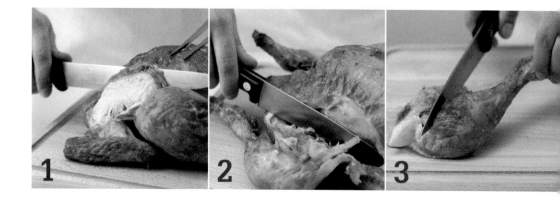

Preparing meat

Whether you are preparing meat for grilling or a joint for roasting, some basic preparation will ensure it has sufficient fat to moisten the meat without making it fatty. For a good texture, some steaks are best tenderised before cooking.

Trimming meat

When preparing meat for cutting into chunks, try to separate the individual muscles, which can be identified by the sinews running between each muscle.

Trimming a joint

1 Cut off the excess fat to leave a thickness of about 5mm (¼ in) – a little fat wil contribute juiciness and flavour. This isn't necessary for very lean cuts.

2 Trim away any stray pieces of meat or sinew left by the butcher.

3 If the joint has a covering of fat, you can lightly score it – taking care not to cut into the meat – to help the fat drain away during cooking.

Tenderising steak

Some cuts of steak benefit from tenderising. There are two ways to do it: by pounding or scoring.

1 To pound, lay the steaks in a single layer on a large piece of clingfilm or waxed paper. Lay another sheet on top of the meat and pound gently with a rolling pin, small frying pan or the flat side of a meat mallet.

2 Scoring is useful for cuts that have long, tough fibres, such as flank. It allows a marinade to penetrate more deeply into the meat. Lay the steak on the chopping board and, using a long, very sharp knife, make shallow cuts in one direction along the whole surface.

3 Make another set of cuts at a 45 degree angle to the first. Turn the meat over and repeat on the other side.

1   2

Roasting and carving meat

The temperature of your oven and the particular cut of meat you have chosen will influence the length of time a roast will take to cook, but these guidelines will help you cook a succulent roast and carve it neatly. For perfect roasting:

Let the meat come to room temperature before cooking – take it out of the refrigerator at least 2 hours ahead of time, 3 hours for a large joint.

Season the joint and flavour with herbs and garlic if you like. Cook on a wire rack, or on a bed of sliced onions, carrots and celery, so that the fat drops away.

Roast fat side up.

Check the pan juices to make sure they don't dry up and scorch; you might need to add water to the roasting tin. The juices can be used to make gravy or a sauce.

When the meat is cooked, loosely cover with foil and leave to rest for 20 minutes before carving (a large joint can rest for 45 minutes without getting cold). It tastes juicier and makes carving easier.

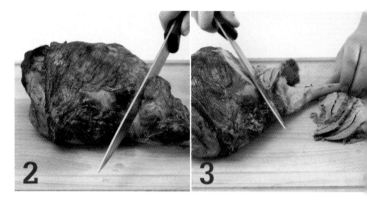

Carving pork with crackling

1 Remove the string and position the carving knife just under the crisp skin. Work the knife under the skin, taking care not to cut into the meat, until you can pull it off with your fingers. Slice the meat then break the crackling into servings.

Carving leg of lamb

1 Hold the shank and cut from that end, holding the knife flat on the bone, a couple of inches into the meat. Cut down on to the bone to remove that chunk and slice thinly.

2 Start cutting thin slices from the meat on the bone, starting at the cut left by the chunk you removed. Hold the knife at right angles to the bone, then cut at a slight angle as you reach the thicker sections of the meat.

3 Carve along that side then turn the leg and continue slicing at an angle until all the meat is removed.

Roasting times

These timings are a rough guide only. They are based on a large joint, such as rib of beef or leg of lamb, brought to room temperature before cooking. Smaller joints may take a little more time – about 3–5 minutes more per 450g (1lb). Check the meat as it nears the end of its cooking time; it may need a few minutes more or less.

	Oven temperature	Timing per 450g (1lb)
Beef		
Rare	160°C (140°C fan oven) mark 3	12-15 minutes
Medium-rare	160°C (140°C fan oven) mark 3	15-18 minutes
Well done	160°C (140°C fan oven) mark 3	20-25 minutes

Lamb		
Medium-rare	180°C (160°C fan) mark 4	15-20 minutes
Well done	180°C (160°C fan) mark 4	20-25 minutes

Pork

If you like, you can give pork a preliminary blast of high heat - 220°C (fan oven 200°C) mark 6 - for 15-20 minutes. If so, watch the pork carefully towards the end of the expected cooking time.

Medium-rare	190°C (170°C fan oven) mark 5	20-25 minutes
Well done	190°C (170°C fan oven) mark 5	25-30 minutes

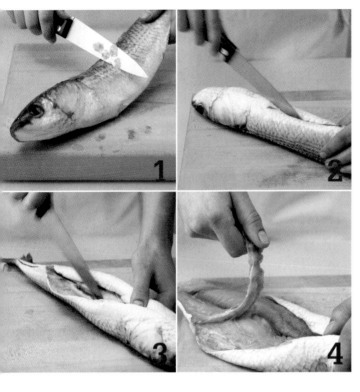

Preparing fish

Most fishmongers will prepare whole fish for you, but it is very simple to clean, bone and fillet them yourself.

Cleaning and boning round fish

1 Cut off the fins with scissors. Using the blunt edge of a knife, scrape the fish from tail to head and rinse off the loose scales. (The scaled fish should feel smooth.)

2 Insert a sharp knife at the hole towards the rear of the stomach and slit the skin up to the gills. Ease out the entrails and use scissors to snip out anything that remains. With the knife, cut along the vein under the backbone. Wash the cavity under running water.

3 Working from the belly side of the fish, cut along one side of the backbone. Remove as many fine bones as possible and separate the backbone from the flesh.

4 Turn the fish over and repeat on the other side. Snip the backbone with scissors, then remove.

Filleting round fish

1 Using a very sharp knife, cut through the flesh down to the backbone just behind the head. Then, working from the head end, insert the knife between the flesh and the ribs on the back of the fish.

2 Holding the knife flat on the ribs, cut all the way down to the tail until the flesh is detached along the full length of the fish.

3 Lift the detached portion of flesh and, with the knife again placed flat on the ribs, cut until the flesh is detached from the bones and remove the fillet.

4 Turn the fish over and repeat on the other side, again working from head to tail, to remove the second fillet from the fish.

Cleaning and skinning flat fish

1 To gut, slit open the skin just behind the head of the fish where the stomach sac begins. Work your fingers in and pull the entrails out, then snip out the remainder with scissors.

2 Thick-skinned fish, such as sole, can be skinned by hand. Make a nick right down to the backbone where the body meets the tail. Work your fingers under the skin until you have lifted enough to get a grip on.

3 Holding the tail in one hand, pull on the skin in the direction of the head. The skin should come away in a single sheet.

4 Thinner-skinned fish can be filleted first, then skinned using a knife. Put the fillet on a board with the skin down and the tail towards you. Make a nick in the tail flesh, just deep enough to cut through to the skin, and lift the little flap of flesh with the knife.

5 Hold the knife on the skin at a very shallow angle, almost parallel to the worksurface, and work it between flesh and skin to remove the skin in a single piece.

Peeling and butterflying prawns

1 To shell prawns, pull off the head (either discard or use later, with the shell, for making stock). Using pointed scissors, cut through the soft shell on the belly side.

2 Prise the shell off, leaving the tail attached.

3 Using a small sharp knife, make a shallow cut along the length of the back of the prawn. Using the point of the knife, carefully remove and discard the black vein (the intestinal tract) that runs along the back of the prawn.

4 To 'butterfly' the prawn, cut halfway through the flesh lengthways from the head end to the base of the tail, and open up the prawn.

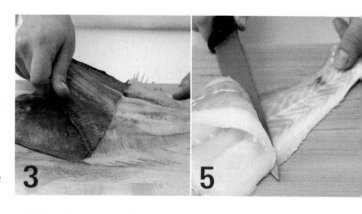

Filleting flat fish

1 Insert a sharp knife between the flesh and ribs on one side of the backbone. Holding the knife nearly parallel to the backbone, cut between the backbone and the flesh until detached. Turn the fish round and repeat on the other side.

2 Turn the fish over and repeat on the other side. Smaller fish may only provide two fillets.

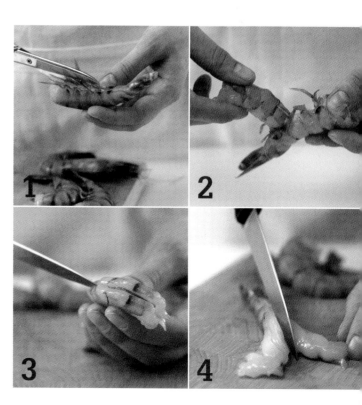

Making stock

Good stock can make the difference between a good dish and a great one. It gives depth of flavour to many dishes. There are four main types of stock: vegetable, meat, chicken and fish.

Stocks

Vegetable stock

For 1.2 litres (2 pints), you will need:
225g (8oz) each onions, celery, leeks and carrots, chopped, 2 bay leaves, a few thyme sprigs, 1 small bunch parsley, 10 black peppercorns, ½ tsp salt.

1 Put all the ingredients in a pan and pour in 1.7 litres (3 pints) cold water.

2 Bring slowly to the boil and skim the surface. Partially cover and simmer for 30 minutes. Adjust the seasoning. Strain the stock through a fine sieve into a bowl and leave to cool.

Meat stock

For 900ml (1½ pints), you will need:
450g (1lb) each meat bones and stewing meat, 1 onion, 2 celery sticks and 1 large carrot, sliced, 1 bouquet garni (2 bay leaves, a few thyme sprigs and a small bunch parsley), 1 tsp black peppercorns, ½ tsp salt.

1 Preheat the oven to 220°C (200°C fan oven) mark 7. Put the meat and bones in a roasting tin and roast for 30–40 minutes, turning now and again, until they are well browned.

2 Put the bones in a large pan with the remaining ingredients and add 2 litres (3½ pints) cold water. Bring slowly to the boil and skim the surface. Partially cover and simmer for 4–5 hours. Adjust the seasoning. Strain through a muslin-lined sieve into a bowl and cool quickly. Degrease (see opposite) before using.

Chicken stock

For 1.2 litres (2 pints), you will need:
1.6kg (3½lb) chicken bones, 225g (8oz) each onions and celery, sliced, 150g (5oz) chopped leeks, 1 bouquet garni (2 bay leaves, a few thyme sprigs and a small bunch parsley), 1 tsp black peppercorns, ½ tsp salt.

1 Put all the ingredients in a large pan with 3 litres (5¼ pints) cold water.

2 Bring slowly to the boil and skim the surface. Partially cover the pan and simmer gently for 2 hours. Adjust the seasoning if necessary.

3 Strain the stock through a muslin-lined sieve into a bowl and cool quickly. Degrease (see right) before using.

Fish stock

For 900ml (1½ pints), you will need:
900g (2lb) fish bones and trimmings, washed, 2 carrots, 1 onion and 2 celery sticks, sliced, 1 bouquet garni (2 bay leaves, a few thyme sprigs and a small bunch parsley), 6 white peppercorns, ½ tsp salt.

1 Put all the ingredients in a large pan with 900ml (1½ pints) cold water. Bring slowly to the boil and skim the surface.

2 Partially cover the pan and simmer gently for 30 minutes. Adjust the seasoning if necessary.

3 Strain through a muslin-lined sieve into a bowl and cool quickly. Fish stock tends not to have much fat in it and so does not usually need to be degreased. However, if it does seem to be fatty, you will need to remove this by degreasing it (see right).

Degreasing stock

Meat and poultry stock needs to be degreased. (Vegetable stock does not.) You can mop the fat from the surface using kitchen paper, but the following methods are easier and more effective. There are three main methods that you can use: ladling, pouring and chilling.

1 **Ladling** While the stock is warm, place a ladle on the surface. Press down to allow the fat floating on the surface to trickle over the edge until the ladle is full. Discard the fat, then repeat until all the fat has been removed.

2 **Pouring** For this you need a degreasing jug or a double-pouring gravy boat, which has the spout at the base of the vessel. When you fill the jug or gravy boat with a fatty liquid, the fat rises. When you pour, the stock comes out while the fat stays behind in the jug.

3 **Chilling** This technique works best with stock made from meat, whose fat solidifies when cold. Put the stock in the refrigerator until the fat becomes solid, then remove the pieces of fat using a slotted spoon.

Food storage and hygiene

Storing food properly and preparing it in a hygienic way is important to ensure that food remains as nutritious and flavourful as possible, and to reduce the risk of food poisoning.

Hygiene

When you are preparing food, always follow these important guidelines:

Wash your hands thoroughly before handling food and again between handling different types of food, such as raw and cooked meat and poultry. If you have any cuts or grazes on your hands, be sure to keep them covered with a waterproof plaster.

Wash down worksurfaces regularly with a mild detergent solution or multi-surface cleaner.

Use a dishwasher if available. Otherwise, wear rubber gloves for washing-up, so that the water temperature can be hotter than unprotected hands can bear. Change drying-up cloths and cleaning cloths regularly. Note that leaving dishes to drain is more hygienic than drying them with a teatowel.

Keep raw and cooked foods separate, especially meat, fish and poultry. Wash kitchen utensils in between preparing raw and cooked foods. Never put cooked or ready-to-eat foods directly on to a surface which has just had raw fish, meat or poultry on it.

Keep pets out of the kitchen if possible; or make sure they stay away from worksurfaces. Never allow animals on to worksurfaces.

Shopping

Always choose fresh ingredients in prime condition from stores and markets that have a regular turnover of stock to ensure you buy the freshest produce possible.

Make sure items are within their 'best before' or 'use by' date. (Foods with a longer shelf life have a 'best before' date; more perishable items have a 'use by' date.)

Pack frozen and chilled items in an insulated cool bag at the check-out and put them into the freezer or refrigerator as soon as you get home.

During warm weather in particular, buy perishable foods just before you return home. When packing items at the check-out, sort them according to where you will store them when you get home – the refrigerator, freezer, storecupboard, vegetable rack, fruit bowl, etc. This will make unpacking easier – and quicker.

The storecupboard

Although storecupboard ingredients will generally last a long time, correct storage is important:

Always check packaging for storage advice – even with familiar foods, because storage requirements may change if additives, sugar or salt have been reduced. Check storecupboard foods for their 'best before' or 'use by' date and do not use them if the date has passed.

Keep all food cupboards scrupulously clean and make sure food containers and packets are properly sealed.

Once opened, treat canned foods as though fresh. Always transfer the contents to a clean container, cover and keep in the refrigerator. Similarly, jars, sauce bottles and cartons should be kept chilled after opening. (Check the label for safe storage times after opening.)

Transfer dry goods such as sugar, rice and pasta to moisture-proof containers. When supplies are used up, wash the container well and thoroughly dry before refilling with new supplies.

Store oils in a dark cupboard away from any heat source as heat and light can make them turn rancid and affect their colour. For the same reason, buy olive oil in dark green bottles.

Store vinegars in a cool place; they can turn bad in a warm environment.

Store dried herbs, spices and flavourings in a cool, dark cupboard or in dark jars. Buy in small quantities as their flavour will not last indefinitely.

Store flours and sugars in airtight containers.

Refrigerator storage

Fresh food needs to be kept in the cool temperature of the refrigerator to keep it in good condition and discourage the growth of harmful bacteria. Store day-to-day perishable items, such as opened jams and jellies, mayonnaise and bottled sauces, in the refrigerator along with eggs and dairy products, fruit juices, bacon, fresh and cooked meat (on separate shelves), and salads and vegetables (except potatoes, which don't suit being stored in the cold). A refrigerator should be kept at an operating temperature of 4–5°C.

It is worth investing in a refrigerator thermometer to ensure the correct temperature is maintained. To ensure your refrigerator is functioning effectively for safe food storage, follow these guidelines:

To avoid bacterial cross-contamination, store cooked and raw foods on separate shelves, putting cooked foods on the top shelf. Ensure that all items are well wrapped.

Never put hot food into the refrigerator, as this will cause the internal temperature of the refrigerator to rise.

Avoid overfilling the refrigerator, as this restricts the circulation of air and prevents the appliance from working properly.

It can take some time for the refrigerator to return to the correct operating temperature once the door has been opened, so don't leave it open any longer than is necessary.

Clean the refrigerator regularly, using a specially formulated germicidal refrigerator cleaner. Alternatively, use a weak solution of bicarbonate of soda: 1 tbsp to 1 litre (1³/₄ pints) water.

If your refrigerator doesn't have an automatic defrost facility, defrost regularly.

Maximum refrigerator storage times

For pre-packed foods, always adhere to the 'use by' date on the packet. For other foods the following storage times should apply, providing the food is in prime condition when it goes into the refrigerator and that your refrigerator is in good working order:

Vegetables and Fruit

Green vegetables	3–4 days
Salad leaves	2–3 days
Hard and stone fruit	3–7 days
Soft fruit	1–2 days

Dairy Food

Cheese, hard	1 week
Cheese, soft	2–3 days
Eggs	1 week
Milk	4–5 days

Fish

Fish	1 day
Shellfish	1 day

Raw Meat

Bacon	7 days
Game	2 days
Joints	3 days
Minced meat	1 day
Offal	1 day
Poultry	2 days
Raw sliced meat	2 days
Sausages	3 days

Cooked Meat

Joints	3 days
Casseroles/stews	2 days
Pies	2 days
Sliced meat	2 days
Ham	2 days
Ham, vacuum-packed (or according to the instructions on the packet)	1–2 weeks

1

Simple Suppers

Try Something Different

The spicy beans are just as good served with toast for a quick meal that takes less than 25 minutes.

Spicy Beans with Jazzed-up Potatoes

4 baking potatoes

1 tbsp olive oil, plus extra to rub

1 tsp smoked paprika, plus a pinch

2 shallots, finely chopped

1 tbsp freshly chopped rosemary

400g can cannellini beans, drained and rinsed

400g can chopped tomatoes

1 tbsp light muscovado sugar

1 tsp Worcestershire sauce

75ml (2$^{1}/_{2}$fl oz) red wine

75ml (2$^{1}/_{2}$fl oz) hot vegetable stock

a small handful of freshly chopped flat-leafed parsley

grated mature Cheddar cheese to sprinkle

salt and ground black pepper

1 Preheat the oven to 200°C (180°C fan oven) mark 6. Rub the baking potatoes with a little oil and put them on a baking tray. Scatter some sea salt over and a pinch of smoked paprika. Bake for 1–1$^{1}/_{2}$ hours.

2 Meanwhile, heat 1 tbsp oil in a large pan, then fry the shallots over a low heat for 1–2 minutes until they start to soften.

3 Add the rosemary and 1 tsp paprika, and fry for 1–2 minutes, then add the beans, tomatoes, sugar, Worcestershire sauce, red wine and stock. Season, then bring to the boil and simmer, uncovered, for 10–15 minutes. Serve with the baked potatoes, scattered with parsley and grated Cheddar cheese.

Serves 4	EASY		NUTRITIONAL INFORMATION	
	Preparation Time 12 minutes	**Cooking Time** about 1$^{1}/_{2}$ hours	**Per Serving** 298 calories, 4g fat (of which 1g saturates), 56g carbohydrate, 0.8g salt	Gluten free

Simple supper menu

▼ Mixed Mushroom Frittata
▶ Fruity Rice Pudding (see page 119)

Mixed Mushroom Frittata

1 tbsp olive oil

300g (11oz) mixed mushrooms, sliced

2 tbsp freshly chopped thyme

zest and juice of $\frac{1}{2}$ lemon

50g (2oz) watercress, chopped

6 medium eggs, beaten

salt and ground black pepper

1 Heat the oil in a large deep frying pan over a medium heat. Add the mushrooms and thyme, and stir-fry for 4–5 minutes until starting to soften and brown. Stir in the lemon zest and juice, then bubble for 1 minute. Lower the heat.

2 Preheat the grill. Add the watercress to the beaten eggs, season with salt and pepper and pour into the pan. Cook on the hob for 7–8 minutes until the sides and base are firm but the centre is still a little soft.

3 Transfer to the grill and cook for 4–5 minutes until just set. Cut into wedges and serve with chunks of stoneground wholegrain bread and a crisp green salad.

EASY		NUTRITIONAL INFORMATION		Serves
Preparation Time 15 minutes	**Cooking Time** 15–20 minutes	**Per Serving** 148 calories, 12g fat (of which 3g saturates), 0g carbohydrate, 0.3g salt	Vegetarian Gluten free • Dairy free	**4**

Simple supper menu

▼ Quick and Easy Carbonara
▶ Strawberry Compote (see page 116)

Quick and Easy Carbonara

350g (12oz) tagliatelle

150g (5oz) smoked bacon, chopped

1 tbsp olive oil

2 large egg yolks

150ml (¼ pint) double cream

50g (2oz) freshly grated Parmesan

2 tbsp freshly chopped parsley

1 Bring a large pan of water to the boil. Add the pasta, bring back to the boil and cook for 4 minutes or according to the packet instructions.

2 Meanwhile, fry the bacon in the oil for 4–5 minutes. Add to the drained pasta and keep hot.

3 Put the egg yolks in a bowl and add the cream. Whisk together. Add to the pasta with the Parmesan and parsley. Toss well.

Serves 4	EASY		NUTRITIONAL INFORMATION
	Preparation Time 5 minutes	**Cooking Time** 10 minutes	**Per Serving** 688 calories, 39g fat (of which 19g saturates), 65g carbohydrate, 1.6g salt

Cook's Tip

This combination of pasta, potatoes, green beans and pesto is a speciality of Liguria on the East coast of Italy. Traditionally, it is made with the twisted pasta shape known as trofie (see photograph) – pieces of pasta are rolled on a flat surface until they form rounded lengths of pasta with tapered ends. Each length is then twisted into its final shape.

Pasta with Pesto and Beans

350g (12oz) trofie or other dried pasta shapes

175g (6oz) fine green beans, roughly chopped

175g (6oz) small salad potatoes, such as Anya, thickly sliced

250g (9oz) fresh pesto sauce

freshly grated Parmesan to serve

1 Bring a large pan of water to the boil. Add the pasta, bring back to the boil and cook for 5 minutes.

2 Add the beans and potatoes to the pan and continue to boil for a further 7–8 minutes until the potatoes are just tender.

3 Drain the pasta, beans and potatoes in a colander, then tip everything back into the pan and stir in the pesto sauce. Serve scattered with freshly grated Parmesan.

EASY		NUTRITIONAL INFORMATION		Serves
Preparation Time 5 minutes	Cooking Time 15 minutes	Per Serving 738 calories, 38g fat (of which 10g saturates), 74g carbohydrate, 1g salt	Vegetarian	4

Spiced Egg Pilau

200g (7oz) basmati or wild rice
150g (5oz) frozen peas
4 medium eggs
200ml (7fl oz) coconut cream
1 tsp mild curry paste
1 tbsp sweet chilli sauce
1 tbsp smooth peanut butter
1 large bunch coriander, roughly chopped
mini poppadums and mango chutney to serve

1 Put the rice into a pan with 450ml (³/₄ pint) boiling water over a low heat and cook for 15 minutes or until just tender. Add the frozen peas for the last 5 minutes of cooking time.

2 Meanwhile, put the eggs into a large pan of boiling water and simmer for 6 minutes, then drain and shell.

3 Put the coconut cream, curry paste, chilli sauce and peanut butter into a small pan and whisk together. Heat the sauce gently, stirring, without allowing it to boil.

4 Drain the rice and stir in the chopped coriander and 2 tbsp of the sauce.

5 Divide the rice among four bowls. Cut the eggs into halves and serve on the rice, spooning the remaining coconut sauce over the top. Serve with the poppadums and chutney.

Serves 4	EASY		NUTRITIONAL INFORMATION	
	Preparation Time 5 minutes	Cooking Time 15 minutes	Per Serving 331 calories, 9g fat (of which 12g saturates), 50g carbohydrate, 0.6g salt	Vegetarian Gluten free • Dairy free

Try Something Different

Use goat's cheese instead of the garlic and herb cheese.

280g pack pizza base mix

2 x 150g packs garlic and herb cheese

12 whole sun-dried tomatoes,
drained of oil and cut into rough pieces

40g (1½oz) pinenuts

12 fresh basil leaves

3 tbsp olive oil

green salad to serve

Garlic Cheese Pizza

1 Put a pizza stone or large baking sheet in the oven and preheat to 220°C (200°C fan oven) mark 7.

2 Mix the pizza base dough according to the packet instructions. On a lightly floured worksurface, knead for a few minutes or until smooth. Roll out to a 33cm (13in) round. Transfer the dough to the preheated pizza stone or baking sheet. Pinch a lip around the edge.

3 Crumble the cheese over the dough and flatten with a palette knife, then sprinkle on the sun-dried tomatoes, pinenuts and basil leaves.

4 Drizzle with the oil and bake for 20–30 minutes until pale golden and cooked to the centre. Serve with a green salad.

EASY	NUTRITIONAL INFORMATION		Serves
Preparation Time 20 minutes	**Cooking Time** 30 minutes	**Per Serving** 536 calories, 30g fat (of which 9g saturates), 54g carbohydrate, 0.6g salt	Vegetarian	**4**

Herby Lemon Fishcakes

900g (2lb) floury potatoes, such as Maris Piper, peeled and quartered

900g (2lb) salmon fillets

juice of 1 lemon

4 tbsp mayonnaise

pinch of cayenne pepper

2 tbsp freshly chopped herbs, such as tarragon, basil or parsley

2 tbsp chilli oil

salt and ground black pepper

lemon wedges to garnish

green salad to serve

1 Put the potatoes in a large pan of cold salted water, cover and bring to the boil. Turn down the heat and simmer for about 20 minutes or until tender. Drain well, put the pan back on the heat to dry the potatoes, then mash.

2 Put the salmon in a pan with 600ml (1 pint) cold water and half the lemon juice. Cover and bring to the boil, then simmer for 1 minute. Turn off the heat and leave to cool in the water for 20–30 minutes.

3 Preheat the oven to 200°C (180°C fan oven) mark 6. Drain the fish, remove the skin and discard, then flake the fish. Add to the potato along with the remaining lemon juice, the mayonnaise, cayenne pepper and chopped herbs. Season and mix together.

4 Line a large baking sheet with foil. Put a 7.5cm (3in) plain cooking ring on the baking sheet and fill with some of the mixture. Lift off, then repeat with the remainder of the mixture to make eight cakes. Drizzle with chilli oil and cook for 25 minutes or until golden. Garnish with lemon wedges and serve with a green salad.

Cook's Tip

If your fishcakes tend to fall apart, put them in the refrigerator for about 2 hours (or 30 minutes in the freezer) before cooking them.

EASY		NUTRITIONAL INFORMATION		Serves
Preparation Time 25 minutes, plus cooling	**Cooking Time** 45 minutes	**Per Serving** 721 calories, 42g fat (of which 7g saturates), 37g carbohydrate, 0.5g salt	Gluten free • Dairy free	4

Crispy Crumbed Fish

50g (2oz) fresh breadcrumbs

a small handful of freshly chopped flat-leafed parsley

2 tbsp capers, chopped

zest of 1 lemon

4 x 150g (5oz) haddock or pollock fillets

½ tbsp Dijon mustard

juice of ½ lemon

salt and ground black pepper

new potatoes and mixed salad to serve

1 Preheat the oven to 180°C (160°C fan oven) mark 4. Put the breadcrumbs into a bowl with the parsley, capers and lemon zest. Mix well, then set aside.

2 Put the fish fillets on a baking tray. Mix the mustard and half the lemon juice in a bowl with a little salt and pepper, then spread over the top of each piece of fish. Spoon the breadcrumb mixture over the top – don't worry if some falls off.

3 Cook in the oven for 10–15 minutes until the fish is cooked and the breadcrumbs are golden. Pour the remaining lemon juice over the top and serve with new potatoes and a mixed salad.

Serves 4	EASY		NUTRITIONAL INFORMATION	
	Preparation Time 5 minutes	**Cooking Time** 10–15 minutes	**Per Serving** 171 calories, 1g fat (of which trace saturates), 10g carbohydrate, 0.8g salt	Dairy free

Try Something Different

Try this with sausages instead of the chicken.
Italian marinade Mix 1 crushed garlic clove with 4 tbsp olive oil, the juice of 1 lemon and 1 tsp dried oregano. If you like, leave to marinate for 1–2 hours before cooking.
Oriental marinade Mix together 2 tbsp soy sauce, 1 tsp demerara sugar, 2 tbsp dry sherry or apple juice, 1 tsp finely chopped fresh root ginger and 1 crushed garlic clove.
Honey and mustard Mix together 2 tbsp grain mustard, 3 tbsp clear honey and the grated zest and juice of 1 lemon.

Sticky Chicken Thighs

1 garlic clove, crushed

1 tbsp clear honey

1 tbsp Thai sweet chilli sauce

4 chicken thighs

rice and green salad to serve

1 Preheat the oven to 200°C (180°C fan oven) mark 6. Put the garlic into a bowl with the honey and chilli sauce, and mix together. Add the chicken thighs and toss to coat.

2 Put into a roasting tin and roast for 15–20 minutes until the chicken is golden and cooked through. Serve with rice and a crisp green salad.

EASY		NUTRITIONAL INFORMATION		Serves
Preparation Time 5 minutes	Cooking Time 20 minutes	Per Serving 218 calories, 12g fat (of which 3g saturates), 5g carbohydrate, 0.4g salt	Gluten free • Dairy free	**4**

Cook's Tip

Sage has a naturally strong, pungent taste, so you only need a little to flavour the chicken. Don't be tempted to add more than just one leaf to each chicken breast as too much will overpower the finished dish.

Stuffed Chicken Breasts

oil to grease
150g (5oz) ball mozzarella
4 chicken breasts, about 150g (5oz) each
4 sage leaves
8 slices Parma ham
new potatoes and steamed spinach to serve

1 Preheat the oven to 200°C (180°C fan oven) mark 6. Lightly grease a baking sheet. Slice the mozzarella into eight, then put two slices on each chicken piece. Top each with a sage leaf.

2 Wrap each piece of chicken in two slices of Parma ham, covering the mozzarella.

3 Put on to the prepared baking sheet and cook in the oven for 20 minutes until the chicken is cooked through. Serve with the potatoes and spinach.

Serves 4	EASY		NUTRITIONAL INFORMATION	
	Preparation Time 5 minutes	**Cooking Time** 20 minutes	**Per Serving** 297 calories, 13g fat (of which 7g saturates), trace carbohydrate, 1.4g salt	Gluten free

SIMPLE SUPPERS **43**

Try Something Different

Use mango instead of the papaya. Make sure it's ripe before you buy it – give it a gentle squeeze to check.
Try the spice rub and fruity relish with pork chops, or with meaty fish such as salmon, swordfish or tuna steaks.

large pinch each of ground cumin and paprika

2 tbsp olive oil

2 tsp light muscovado sugar

8 thin smoked gammon steaks, about 125g (4oz) each

2 large ripe papayas

zest and juice of 2 limes

½ red chilli, seeded and finely chopped (see page 82)

20g (¾oz) fresh mint, finely chopped

steamed green beans to serve

Cumin-spiced Gammon

1 Preheat the grill. In a small bowl, mix together the cumin, paprika, oil and half the sugar. Put the gammon on to a non-stick baking sheet, then brush the spiced oil over each side.

2 Grill the gammon for about 5 minutes on each side, basting once or twice with the juices.

3 Meanwhile, cut each papaya in half, then deseed and peel. Roughly chop half the flesh and put into a bowl. Purée the remaining fruit with the lime juice. Add to the bowl with the lime zest, chilli, mint and remaining sugar. Spoon the mixture on top of the gammon and serve with green beans.

EASY		NUTRITIONAL INFORMATION		Serves
Preparation Time 10 minutes	**Cooking Time** 10 minutes	**Per Serving** 492 calories, 18g fat (of which 5g saturates), 3g carbohydrate, 13.8g salt	Gluten free • Dairy free	**4**

Simple supper menu

▼ American Sticky Ribs
▶ Fruit Kebabs with Spiced Pear Dip
  (see page 111)

900g (2lb) lean pork spare ribs

125g (4oz) hoisin sauce

2 tbsp mild clear honey

2 tsp English mustard

3 tsp white wine or cider vinegar

4 tbsp tomato ketchup

2 garlic cloves, crushed

4 tbsp fresh apple or orange juice

coleslaw, onion rings and orange wedges to serve

American Sticky Ribs

1 Preheat the oven to 200°C (180°C fan oven) mark 6. Line a large tin with a double layer of foil and spread the ribs over the base.

2 Whisk together the remaining ingredients in a bowl, then spoon over the pork – it may look as though there isn't enough liquid but the ribs will release plenty of juices as they cook.

3 Cover with foil and cook for 20 minutes. Turn the ribs over, then put back in the oven, uncovered. Cook for 40–45 minutes, basting occasionally, until they are dark golden and sticky, and most of the liquid has gone. Serve hot, with coleslaw, onion rings and orange wedges.

Serves 4	EASY		NUTRITIONAL INFORMATION	
	Preparation Time 10 minutes	Cooking Time about 1 hour	Per Serving 485 calories, 30g fat (of which 12g saturates), 12g carbohydrate, 1.3g salt	Dairy free

Cook's Tip

Make your own mint sauce: finely chop 20g (³/₄oz) fresh mint and mix with 1 tbsp each olive oil and white wine vinegar.

Lamb Chops with Crispy Garlic Potatoes

2 tbsp mint sauce

8 small lamb chops

3 medium potatoes, peeled and cut into 5mm (¹/₄ in) slices

2 tbsp garlic-flavoured olive oil

1 tbsp olive oil

salt and ground black pepper

steamed green beans to serve

1 Spread the mint sauce over the lamb chops and leave to marinate while you prepare the potatoes.

2 Boil the potatoes in a pan of lightly salted water for 2 minutes until just starting to soften. Drain, tip back into the pan, season and toss through the garlic oil.

3 Meanwhile, heat the olive oil in a large frying pan and fry the chops for 4–5 minutes on each side until just cooked, adding a splash of boiling water to the pan to make a sauce. Remove the chops and sauce from the pan and keep warm.

4 Add the potatoes to the pan. Fry over a medium heat for 10–12 minutes until crisp and golden. Divide the potatoes, chops and sauce among four plates and serve with green beans.

EASY		NUTRITIONAL INFORMATION		Serves
Preparation Time 10 minutes	**Cooking Time** 20 minutes	**Per Serving** 835 calories, 45g fat (of which 19g saturates), 22g carbohydrate, 0.7g salt	Gluten free • Dairy free	**4**

Quick Steak Supper

2 sirloin steaks

3 tsp olive oil

4 large mushrooms, sliced

1 red onion, sliced

1 tbsp Dijon mustard

25g (1oz) butter

2 ciabattas, halved lengthways, then quartered, to make eight pieces

salt and ground black pepper

green salad to serve

1 Heat a griddle or large frying pan until very hot. Rub the steaks with 1 tsp olive oil, season with salt and pepper, and fry for about 2 minutes on each side if you like your steak rare, or 4 minutes each side for medium. Remove from the pan and leave to 'rest'.

2 Heat the remaining olive oil in the pan. Add the sliced mushrooms and red onion. Fry, stirring, for 5 minutes until softened. Stir in the Dijon mustard and butter, and take off the heat.

3 Toast the ciabatta pieces on both sides. Thinly slice the steaks and divide among four pieces of ciabatta. Top with the mushrooms, onion and remaining ciabatta and serve with a green salad.

Try Something Different

Instead of ciabatta, serve the steak with tagliatelle or other pasta.

Serves 4	EASY		NUTRITIONAL INFORMATION
	Preparation Time 10 minutes	**Cooking Time** 10 minutes	**Per Serving** 452 calories, 17g fat (of which 6g saturates), 44g carbohydrate, 1.6g salt

2

Light and Healthy

Pea and Watercress Soup

75g (3oz) butter

175g (6oz) watercress

10–12 spring onions

700g (1½lb) baking potatoes, peeled and roughly chopped

225g (8oz) frozen petits pois

1.7 litres (3 pints) hot vegetable stock

150ml (¼ pint) double cream

salt and ground black pepper

1 Melt the butter in a large pan, then add the watercress and spring onions, snipping them into rough pieces with scissors as you drop them into the pan. Cook gently over a low heat for 10 minutes.

2 Add the potatoes to the pan with the peas and most of the stock. Cover, bring to the boil, then simmer gently for 20–25 minutes until the potatoes are very tender.

3 Pour in the cream, then season to taste with salt and pepper.

4 Purée the soup in the pan with a stick blender, or leave to cool, then purée in a blender. Add a little extra stock if the soup is too thick.

5 Warm the soup through to serve – but don't boil it or the cream will split.

Freezing Tip

Complete the recipe to end of step 4, then put into a freezerproof container, cool, label and freeze for up to one month.
To use Thaw and complete the recipe.

EASY		NUTRITIONAL INFORMATION		Serves
Preparation Time 20 minutes	**Cooking Time** 30–35 minutes	**Per Serving** 251 calories, 18g fat (of which 11g saturates), 18g carbohydrate, 1g salt	Vegetarian Gluten free	**8**

Try Something Different

Serve this broth with 2 tsp pesto added to each bowl and chunks of crusty bread.

Spring Vegetable Broth

1 tbsp olive oil

4 shallots, chopped

1 fennel bulb, chopped

1 leek, chopped

5 small carrots, chopped

1.1 litres (2 pints) hot vegetable or chicken stock

2 courgettes, chopped

1 bunch asparagus, chopped

2 x 400g cans cannellini beans, drained and rinsed

50g (2oz) Gruyère or Parmesan shavings to serve

1 Heat the oil in a large pan. Add the shallots, fennel, leek and carrots, and fry for 5 minutes or until they start to soften.

2 Add the stock, cover and bring to the boil. Add the courgettes, asparagus and beans, then simmer for 5–6 minutes until the vegetables are tender. Ladle into bowls and sprinkle with a little cheese.

Serves 4	EASY		NUTRITIONAL INFORMATION	
	Preparation Time 20 minutes	**Cooking Time** about 15 minutes	**Per Serving** 315 calories, 9g fat (of which 3g saturates), 40g carbohydrate, 2.9g salt	Vegetarian Gluten free

Roast Mushrooms with Pesto

8 portobello mushrooms

8 tbsp fresh pesto

toasted ciabatta, salad and basil leaves to serve

1 Preheat the oven to 200°C (180°C fan oven) mark 6. Put the mushrooms into an ovenproof dish, then spoon 1 tbsp fresh pesto on top of each one.

2 Pour 150ml (¼ pint) boiling water into the tin, then cook for 15 minutes until the mushrooms are soft and the topping is hot. Serve with toasted ciabatta and salad, and scatter a few small basil leaves over.

EASY		NUTRITIONAL INFORMATION		Serves
Preparation Time 5 minutes	**Cooking Time** 15 minutes	**Per Serving** 258 calories, 23g fat (of which 6g saturates), 1g carbohydrate, 0.5g salt	Vegetarian	**4**

Creamy Baked Eggs

butter to grease

4 sun-dried tomatoes

4 medium eggs

4 tbsp double cream

salt and ground black pepper

Granary bread to serve

1 Preheat the oven to 180°C (160°C fan oven) mark 4. Grease four individual ramekins.

2 Put 1 tomato in each ramekin and season with salt and pepper. Carefully break an egg on top of each, then drizzle 1 tbsp cream over each egg.

3 Bake for 15–18 minutes – the eggs will continue to cook once they have been taken out of the oven.

4 Leave to stand for 2 minutes before serving. Serve with Granary bread.

Serves 4	EASY		NUTRITIONAL INFORMATION	
	Preparation Time 5 minutes	**Cooking Time** 15–18 minutes	**Per Serving** 153 calories, 14g fat (of which 7g saturates), 1g carbohydrate, 0.2g salt	Vegetarian Gluten free

Cook's Tip

For a substantial brunch, serve the piperade with chunks of crusty baguette.

Piperade

2 tbsp olive oil

1 medium onion, finely chopped

1 garlic clove, finely chopped

1 red pepper, seeded and chopped

375g (13oz) tomatoes, peeled, seeded and chopped

pinch of cayenne pepper

8 large eggs

salt and ground black pepper

freshly chopped flat-leafed parsley to garnish

1 Heat the oil in a heavy-based frying pan. Add the onion and garlic, and cook gently for 5 minutes. Add the red pepper and cook for 10 minutes or until softened.

2 Add the tomatoes, increase the heat and cook until they are reduced to a thick pulp. Season well with cayenne pepper, salt and pepper.

3 Lightly whisk the eggs and add to the frying pan. Using a wooden spoon, stir gently until they've just begun to set but are still creamy. Garnish with parsley and serve immediately.

EASY		NUTRITIONAL INFORMATION		Serves
Preparation Time 20 minutes	**Cooking Time** 20 minutes	**Per Serving** 245 calories, 17g fat (of which 4g saturates), 10g carbohydrate, 0.4g salt	Vegetarian Gluten free • Dairy free	**4**

Gazpacho with Tortilla Chips

900g (2lb) ripe tomatoes
4 garlic cloves
50g (2oz) fresh white breadcrumbs
6 tbsp extra virgin olive oil
juice of 1½ small limes
1 red chilli, seeded and chopped (see page 82)
2 cucumbers, seeded and chopped
2 bunches spring onions, chopped
1 red pepper, seeded and chopped
600ml (1 pint) tomato juice
6 tbsp freshly chopped coriander
salt and ground black pepper
175g bag tortilla chips to serve

To garnish
1 large avocado
juice of ½ small lime
150ml (¼ pint) soured cream
a few fresh coriander sprigs

1 Score a cross in the skin at the base of each tomato, then put into a bowl. Pour over enough boiling water to cover them, leave for 30 seconds, then transfer to a bowl of cold water. Peel, discarding the skins, then cut into quarters. Discard the seeds.

2 Put all the gazpacho ingredients into a large bowl and mix well, then whiz together in batches in a food processor until smooth, and transfer to a bowl or jug. Season generously with salt and pepper and stir the soup well. Cover and chill for at least 2 hours or overnight.

3 Just before serving, peel and roughly dice the avocado, then toss in lime juice to coat. Serve the soup garnished with soured cream, the avocado, a sprinkling of black pepper and fresh coriander. Serve the tortilla chips separately.

Cook's Tip

Don't be tempted to make the garnish too far in advance, as the delicate pale green flesh of avocado discolours when exposed to air.

Serves	EASY		NUTRITIONAL INFORMATION	
8	**Preparation Time** 25–30 minutes, plus 2 hours or overnight chilling		**Per Serving** 303 calories, 20g fat (of which 5g saturates), 28g carbohydrate, 1.1g salt	Vegetarian

Try Something Different

There are lots of alternatives to cod: try sea bass, gurnard or pollack.

Oven-poached Cod with Herbs

10 spring onions, sliced

2 garlic cloves, crushed

6 tbsp shredded fresh mint

6 tbsp freshly chopped flat-leafed parsley

juice of $\frac{1}{2}$ lemon

150ml ($\frac{1}{4}$ pint) fish, chicken or vegetable stock

4 cod fillets, about 200g (7oz) each

salt and ground black pepper

lemon wedges to garnish

mashed potatoes to serve

1 Preheat the oven to 230°C (210°C fan oven) mark 8. Combine the spring onions (putting some of the green part to one side), garlic, mint, parsley, lemon juice and stock in an ovenproof dish that can hold the cod in a single layer.

2 Put the cod on the herb and garlic mixture, and turn to moisten. Season with salt and pepper, and roast for 8–10 minutes.

3 Sprinkle with the reserved spring onion, garnish with lemon wedges and serve with mashed potatoes.

Serves 4	EASY		NUTRITIONAL INFORMATION	
	Preparation Time 10 minutes	**Cooking Time** 10 minutes	**Per Serving** 170 calories, 2g fat (of which trace saturates), 1g carbohydrate, 0.5g salt	Gluten free • Dairy free

Try Something Different

Use chopped black olives instead of capers.

Mediterranean Chicken

1 red pepper, seeded and chopped

2 tbsp capers

2 tbsp freshly chopped rosemary

2 tbsp olive oil

4 skinless chicken breasts

salt and ground black pepper

rice or new potatoes to serve

1 Preheat the oven to 200°C (180°C fan oven) mark 6. Put the red pepper in a bowl with the capers, rosemary and oil. Season with salt and pepper and mix well.

2 Put the chicken breasts into an ovenproof dish and spoon the pepper mixture over the top. Roast for 15–20 minutes until the chicken is cooked through and the topping is hot. Serve with rice or new potatoes.

EASY		NUTRITIONAL INFORMATION		Serves
Preparation Time 5 minutes	**Cooking Time** 20 minutes	**Per Serving** 223 calories, 7g fat (of which 1g saturates), 3g carbohydrate, 0.2g salt	Gluten free • Dairy free	**4**

Chicken Stir-fry with Noodles

2 tbsp vegetable oil

2 garlic cloves, crushed

4 skinless, boneless chicken breasts, each sliced into 10 pieces

3 medium carrots, about 450g (1lb), cut into thin strips, about 5cm (2in) long

250g pack thick egg noodles

1 bunch spring onions, sliced

200g (7oz) mangetouts, ends trimmed

155g jar sweet chilli and lemongrass sauce

1 Fill a large pan with water and bring to the boil. Meanwhile, heat the oil in a wok or frying pan, then add the garlic and stir-fry for 1–2 minutes. Add the chicken pieces and stir-fry for 5 minutes, then add the carrot strips and stir-fry for a further 5 minutes.

2 Put the noodles into the boiling water and cook according to the packet instructions.

3 Meanwhile, add the spring onions, mangetouts and sauce to the wok. Stir-fry for 5 minutes.

4 Drain the cooked noodles well and add to the wok. Toss everything together and serve.

Try Something Different

Use turkey or pork escalopes instead of the chicken: you will need 450g (1lb), cut into thin strips.

EASY		NUTRITIONAL INFORMATION		Serves
Preparation Time 20 minutes	**Cooking Time** 20 minutes	**Per Serving** 355 calories, 10g fat (of which 1.5g saturates), 29g carbohydrate, 0.5g salt	Dairy free	**4**

Try Something Different

Use Gruyère or Emmenthal instead of Cheddar.
Add freshly chopped chives or parsley.
Sprinkle with 1 tbsp mixed seeds just before serving.

Cheese Coleslaw with Roast Chicken

1 baby white cabbage, thinly shredded

4 spring onions, finely chopped

1 large carrot, finely shredded

75g (3oz) mature Cheddar cheese, grated

6 tbsp mayonnaise

ground black pepper

cress to garnish

sliced roast chicken to serve

1 In a large bowl, mix together the white cabbage, spring onions, carrot, cheese and mayonnaise. Season with pepper.

2 Divide among four small bowls or plates and snip some cress over. Serve with slices of roast chicken.

Serves	EASY		NUTRITIONAL INFORMATION	
4	**Preparation Time** 15 minutes		**Per Serving** 270 calories, 23g fat (of which 7g saturates), 8g carbohydrate, 0.6g salt	Gluten free

Cook's Tip

For vinaigrette dressing, whisk 1 tsp Dijon mustard with a pinch of sugar, 1 tbsp white wine vinegar, and salt and pepper in a bowl. Gradually whisk in 6 tbsp extra virgin olive oil until well combined. Alternatively, shake all the ingredients together in a screw-topped jar.

Peach Couscous and Mustard Sauce with Ham

175g (6oz) couscous

2 large ripe peaches, halved, stoned and roughly chopped

300ml (½ pint) hot vegetable stock

3 tbsp freshly chopped parsley

100g (3½ oz) mixed dried fruit, nuts and seeds, such as cranberries, almonds, pecan nuts and pumpkin seeds

2 tbsp vinaigrette dressing (see Cook's Tip)

2 tbsp mayonnaise

2 tsp Dijon mustard

2 tsp freshly chopped dill, plus extra sprigs to garnish

salt and ground black pepper

smoked ham to serve

1 Put the couscous into a large bowl. Add the peaches and pour in the stock. Cover and set aside for 5 minutes until the liquid has been absorbed.

2 Stir the chopped parsley, dried fruit, nuts and seeds and vinaigrette dressing into the couscous. Season with salt and pepper.

3 Put the mayonnaise in a bowl and mix with 1 tbsp water and the mustard and dill. Serve the couscous with smoked ham and a spoonful of mustard sauce, garnished with dill sprigs.

EASY	NUTRITIONAL INFORMATION		Serves
Preparation Time 15 minutes	**Per Serving** 349 calories, 19g fat (of which 2g saturates), 38g carbohydrate, 0.5g salt	Dairy free	**4**

Bacon and Egg Salad

4 medium eggs
250g (9oz) rindless smoked bacon
150g (5oz) cherry tomatoes
2 slices thick-cut bread
3 tbsp mayonnaise
½ lemon
25g (1oz) freshly grated Parmesan
2 Little Gem lettuces
ground black pepper

1 Heat a pan of water until simmering, add the eggs and boil for 6 minutes. Cool completely under cold water, peel and set to one side.

2 Meanwhile, heat a griddle pan, then fry the bacon for 5 minutes until crisp. Remove from the pan and chop into large pieces. Leave to cool.

3 Add the tomatoes and bread to the pan and fry in the bacon juices for 2–3 minutes until the bread is crisp and the tomatoes are starting to char. Remove from the heat, chop the bread into bite-sized croûtons and set to one side.

4 To make the dressing, put the mayonnaise into a bowl and squeeze in the lemon juice. Add the Parmesan to the bowl and mix. Season with pepper.

5 Separate the Little Gem leaves and put into a large serving bowl. Cut the eggs in half and add to the bowl with the bacon, tomatoes and croûtons. Drizzle the dressing over, toss lightly and serve.

Light and healthy menu

▲ Bacon and Egg Salad
▶ Elderflower and Fruit Jelly (see page 112)

Serves	EASY		NUTRITIONAL INFORMATION
4	**Preparation Time** 10 minutes	**Cooking Time** 10 minutes	**Per Serving** 360 calories, 27g fat (of which 8g saturates), 9g carbohydrate, 3.1g salt

3

Hearty Warmers

Hearty warmer menu

▼ Lamb and Pasta Pot
▶ Lemon and Passion Fruit Fool
   (see page 113)

Lamb and Pasta Pot

1 half leg of lamb roasting joint – about
1.1kg (2½lb) total weight

125g (4oz) smoked streaky bacon, chopped

150ml (¼ pint) red wine

400g can chopped tomatoes with chilli, or passata

75g (3oz) dried pasta shapes

12 sunblush tomatoes

150g (5oz) chargrilled artichokes in oil, drained
and halved

a handful of basil leaves to garnish

1 Preheat the oven to 200°C (180°C fan oven) mark 6. Put the lamb and bacon in a small, deep roasting tin and fry for 5 minutes or until the lamb is brown all over and the bacon is beginning to crisp.

2 Remove the lamb and set aside. Pour the wine into the tin with the bacon – it should bubble immediately. Stir well, scraping the base to loosen any crusty bits, then leave to bubble until half the wine has evaporated. Stir in 300ml (½ pint) water and add the chopped tomatoes or passata, pasta and sunblush tomatoes.

3 Put the lamb on a rack over the roasting tin so that the juices drip into the pasta. Cook, uncovered, in the oven for about 35 minutes.

4 Stir the artichokes into the pasta and put everything back in the oven for 5 minutes or until the lamb is tender and the pasta cooked. Slice the lamb thickly. Serve with the pasta and scatter the basil on top.

Serves 4	EASY		NUTRITIONAL INFORMATION	
	Preparation Time 10 minutes	**Cooking Time** 50 minutes	**Per Serving** 686 calories, 36g fat (of which 16g saturates), 18g carbohydrate, 1.4g salt	Dairy free

Cook's Tip

Italian Dolcelatte cheese has a much milder flavour than Stilton or Roquefort; it also has a deliciously rich, creamy texture.

125g (4oz) fresh or frozen leaf spinach, thawed

40g (1½oz) fresh basil, roughly chopped

250g (9oz) ricotta cheese

5 pieces marinated artichokes, drained and chopped

350g carton cheese sauce

175g (6oz) Dolcelatte cheese, roughly diced

9 sheets fresh egg lasagne

25g (1oz) pinenuts, toasted

tomato salad to serve

Spinach and Cheese Lasagne

1 Preheat the oven to 180°C (160°C fan oven) mark 4. Chop the spinach finely (if it was frozen, squeeze out the excess liquid first). Put in a bowl with the basil, ricotta cheese, artichokes and 6 tbsp cheese sauce. Mix well.

2 Beat the Dolcelatte into the remaining cheese sauce. Layer the ricotta mixture, lasagne, then cheese sauce into a 23 x 23cm (9 x 9in) ovenproof dish. Repeat to use up the remainder.

3 Cook the lasagne for 40 minutes. Sprinkle over the pinenuts and put back in the oven for a further 10–15 minutes until golden. Serve with a tomato salad.

EASY		NUTRITIONAL INFORMATION		Serves
Preparation Time 30 minutes	**Cooking Time** 50–55 minutes	**Per Serving** 442 calories, 27g fat (of which 14g saturates), 32g carbohydrate, 1.6g salt	Vegetarian	**6**

Stuffed Pasta Shells

2 tbsp olive oil

1 large onion, finely chopped

a few fresh rosemary or oregano sprigs, chopped

125g (4oz) small flat mushrooms, sliced

6 plump coarse sausages, skinned

175ml (6fl oz) red wine

300ml (½ pint) passata

4 tbsp sun-dried tomato paste

sugar to taste, if necessary

250g (9oz) large dried pasta shells, such as conchiglioni rigati

150ml (¼ pint) half-fat single cream (optional)

freshly grated Parmesan to garnish

green salad to serve

1 Preheat the oven to 180°C (160°C fan oven) mark 4. Heat the oil in a deep frying pan. Stir in the onion and rosemary or oregano and cook over a gentle heat for 10 minutes or until the onion is soft and golden. Add the mushrooms and cook over a medium heat until the vegetables are soft and beginning to brown at the edges. Tip the onion mixture into a bowl.

2 Crumble the sausagemeat into the hot pan and stir over a high heat with a wooden spoon, breaking the meat up as you do so, until browned all over. Reduce the heat slightly and pour in the wine. Leave to bubble and reduce by about half. Return the onion mixture to the pan and add the passata and sun-dried tomato paste. Bubble gently for another 10 minutes. Add a pinch of sugar if the sauce tastes a little sharp.

3 While the sauce is simmering, cook the pasta shells in plenty of boiling water for 10 minutes or until just tender. Drain well and run under the cold tap to cool.

4 Fill the shells with the sauce and put in a shallow ovenproof dish. Drizzle over any extra sauce and the cream, if using, and bake for 30 minutes or until piping hot. Sprinkle with Parmesan and serve with a big bowl of green salad.

Try Something Different

Turkey or chicken mince would make a lighter alternative to the sausages: you will need 450g (1lb).
Use a small aubergine, diced, instead of the mushrooms.

Serves	EASY		NUTRITIONAL INFORMATION
6	Preparation Time 15 minutes	Cooking Time about 1 hour	Per Serving 378 calories, 17g fat (of which 5g saturates), 41g carbohydrate, 1.1g salt

Italian Meatballs

50g (2oz) fresh breadcrumbs

450g (1lb) minced lean pork

1 tsp fennel seeds, crushed

¼ tsp chilli flakes, or to taste

3 garlic cloves, crushed

4 tbsp freshly chopped flat-leafed parsley

3 tbsp red wine

oil-water spray

salt and ground black pepper

roughly chopped fresh oregano to garnish

spaghetti to serve

For the tomato sauce

oil-water spray

2 large shallots, finely chopped

3 pitted black olives, shredded

2 garlic cloves, crushed

2 pinches of chilli flakes

250ml (9fl oz) vegetable or chicken stock

500g carton passata

2 tbsp each freshly chopped flat-leafed parsley, basil and oregano

1 To make the tomato sauce, spray a pan with the oil-water spray and add the shallots. Cook gently for 5 minutes. Add the olives, garlic, chilli flakes and stock. Bring to the boil, cover and simmer for 3–4 minutes.

2 Uncover and simmer for 10 minutes or until the shallots and garlic are soft and the liquid syrupy. Stir in the passata and season with salt and pepper. Bring to the boil and simmer for 10–15 minutes, then stir in the herbs.

3 Meanwhile, put the breadcrumbs and remaining ingredients into a large bowl, season and mix together, using your hands, until thoroughly combined. (If you wish to check the seasoning, fry a little mixture, taste and adjust if necessary.)

4 With wet hands, roll the mixture into balls. Line a grill pan with foil, shiny side up, and spray with the oil-water spray. Cook the meatballs under a preheated grill for 3–4 minutes on each side. Serve with the tomato sauce and spaghetti, garnished with oregano.

EASY		NUTRITIONAL INFORMATION		Serves
Preparation Time 15 minutes	**Cooking Time** 50 minutes	**Per Serving** 275 calories, 12g fat (of which 4g saturates), 16g carbohydrate, 1.8g salt	Dairy free	**4**

Freezing Tip

Prepare the fish mixture to step 3, then put into a freezerproof container, cool, label and freeze for up to one month.
To use Thaw and complete the recipe.

700g (1½lb) floury potatoes, such as Maris Piper, peeled and chopped

25g (1oz) butter

1 tbsp plain flour

½ onion, finely sliced

75ml (3fl oz) double cream

150ml (¼ pint) hot vegetable stock

a splash of white wine (optional)

15g (½oz) freshly grated Parmesan

2 tsp Dijon mustard

350g (12oz) undyed skinless smoked haddock, roughly chopped

150g (5oz) frozen peas

salt and ground black pepper

Smoked Fish Pie

1   Put the potatoes into a pan of cold salted water and bring to the boil. Simmer for 15–20 minutes until tender. Drain well, tip back into the pan, then mash with 15g (½oz) butter. Season with salt and pepper.

2   Preheat the oven to 220°C (200°C fan) mark 7. Heat the remaining butter in a large pan, add the flour and onion, and cook for 10 minutes or until the onion is soft and golden. Add the cream, stock, wine, if using, Parmesan and mustard. Stir everything together and season.

3   Add the fish and peas, and turn off the heat. Stir the mixture carefully.

4   Put the fish mixture into a 2.3 litre (4 pint) ovenproof dish. Cover with the mash, then cook in the oven for 15–20 minutes until the fish is cooked through.

Serves 4	EASY		NUTRITIONAL INFORMATION
	Preparation Time 15 minutes	**Cooking Time** 40–50 minutes	**Per Serving** 403 calories, 18g fat (of which 11g saturates), 37g carbohydrate, 2.1g salt

Try Something Different

There are lots of alternatives to cod and haddock: try sea bass, gurnard, coley (saithe) or pollack.

Fish Stew

2 tbsp olive oil

1 onion, chopped

1 leek, chopped

2 tsp smoked paprika

2 tbsp tomato purée

450g (1lb) cod or haddock, roughly chopped

125g (4oz) basmati rice

175ml (6fl oz) white wine

450ml (¾ pint) hot fish stock

200g (7oz) cooked, peeled king prawns

a large handful of spinach leaves

crusty bread to serve

1 Heat the oil in a large pan. Add the onion and leek and fry for 8–10 minutes until they start to soften. Add the smoked paprika and tomato purée, and cook for 1–2 minutes.

2 Add the fish, rice, wine and stock. Bring to the boil, then cover and simmer for 10 minutes or until the fish is cooked through and the rice is tender. Add the prawns, cook for 1 minute until heated through, stir in the spinach and serve with chunks of bread.

EASY		NUTRITIONAL INFORMATION		Serves
Preparation Time 15 minutes	**Cooking Time** about 30 minutes	**Per Serving** 280 calories, 7g fat (of which 1g saturates), 34g carbohydrate, 0.3g salt	Gluten free • Dairy free	**4**

Spicy Pork and Bean Stew

3 tbsp olive oil

400g (14oz) pork escalopes, cubed

1 red onion, sliced

2 leeks, cut into chunks

2 celery sticks, cut into chunks

1 tbsp harissa paste

1 tbsp tomato purée

400g (14oz) cherry tomatoes

300ml (½ pint) hot vegetable or chicken stock

400g can cannellini beans, drained and rinsed

1 marinated red pepper, sliced

salt and ground black pepper

freshly chopped flat-leafed parsley to garnish

Greek yogurt, lemon wedges and bread to serve

1 Preheat the oven to 180°C (160°C fan oven) mark 4. Heat 2 tbsp oil in a flameproof casserole and fry the pork in batches until golden. Remove from the pan and set aside.

2 Heat the remaining oil in the pan and fry the onion for 5–10 minutes until softened. Add the leeks and celery, and cook for about 5 minutes. Return the pork to the pan, and add the harissa and tomato purée. Cook for 1–2 minutes, stirring all the time. Add the tomatoes and stock and season well with salt and pepper. Bring to the boil, then transfer to the oven and cook for 25 minutes.

3 Add the drained beans and red pepper to the mixture and put back in the oven for 5 minutes to warm through. Garnish with parsley and serve with a dollop of Greek yogurt, lemon wedges for squeezing over, and chunks of crusty baguette or wholegrain bread.

Serves 4	EASY		NUTRITIONAL INFORMATION	
	Preparation Time 15 minutes	**Cooking Time** 50–55 minutes	**Per Serving** 348 calories, 14g fat (of which 3g saturates), 27g carbohydrate, 1.5g salt	Gluten free • Dairy free

Try Something Different

For a vegetarian alternative, leave out the ham and use 250g (9oz) cheese. Add three-quarters of the cheese over the first layer of bread and scatter the remaining cheese on top.

150–175g (5–6oz) thickly sliced white bread (such as sourdough), crusts left on

75g (3oz) butter, softened

Dijon mustard

200g (7oz) sliced ham, very roughly chopped

150g (5oz) mature Cheddar cheese, grated

575ml (19½fl oz) full-fat milk

5 large eggs, beaten

pinch of freshly grated nutmeg

2 tbsp freshly chopped herbs, such as parsley, marjoram or thyme

salt and ground black pepper

green salad to serve

Savoury Pudding

1 Spread the bread generously with butter and sparingly with mustard. Put half the slices in the base of a 2 litre (3½ pint) ovenproof dish. Top with the ham and half the cheese, then with the remaining bread, butter side up. Whisk together the milk, eggs, nutmeg and plenty of salt and pepper. Stir in the herbs, then slowly pour the mixture over the bread. Scatter the remaining cheese on top and leave to soak for 15 minutes. Meanwhile, preheat the oven to 180°C (160°C fan oven) mark 4.

2 Put the dish in a roasting tin and fill halfway up the sides with hand-hot water, then cook for 1–1¼ hours until puffed up, golden brown and just set to the centre. Serve immediately, with a green salad.

EASY		NUTRITIONAL INFORMATION	Serves
Preparation Time 15 minutes, plus 15 minutes soaking	**Cooking Time** 1–1¼ hours	**Per Serving** 397 calories, 27g fat (of which 15g saturates), 17g carbohydrate, 2.2g salt	**6**

Chicken with Chorizo and Beans

1 tbsp olive oil

12 chicken pieces (6 drumsticks and 6 thighs)

175g (6oz) Spanish chorizo sausage, cubed

1 onion, finely chopped

2 large garlic cloves, crushed

1 tsp mild chilli powder

3 red Romano peppers, cut in half, seeded and very roughly chopped

400g (14oz) passata

2 tbsp tomato purée

300ml (½ pint) chicken stock

2 x 400g cans butter beans, drained and rinsed

200g (7oz) baby new potatoes, halved

1 small bunch thyme

1 bay leaf

200g (7oz) baby leaf spinach

1 Preheat the oven to 190°C (170°C fan oven) mark 5. Heat the oil in a large flameproof casserole and brown the chicken all over. Remove from the pan and set aside. Add the chorizo to the casserole and fry for 2–3 minutes until its oil starts to run.

2 Add the onion, garlic and chilli powder, and fry over a low heat for 5 minutes or until soft.

3 Add the peppers and cook for 2–3 minutes until soft. Stir in the passata, tomato purée, stock, beans, potatoes, thyme sprigs and bay leaf. Cover and simmer for 10 minutes.

4 Return the chicken and any juices to the casserole. Bring to a simmer, then cover and cook in the oven for 30–35 minutes. If the sauce looks thin, return the casserole to the hob over a medium heat and simmer to reduce until nicely thick.

5 Remove the thyme and bay leaf, and stir in the spinach until it wilts. Serve the casserole immediately.

Try Something Different

Use mixed beans instead of the butter beans.

EASY			NUTRITIONAL INFORMATION		Serves
Preparation Time 10 minutes	**Cooking Time** about 1 hour 10 minutes		**Per Serving** 690 calories, 41g fat (of which 12g saturates), 33g carbohydrate, 2.6g salt	Dairy free	**6**

> **Hearty warmer menu**
> ▼ Chicken with Peperonata Sauce
> ▶ Apples with Butterscotch Sauce
>   (see page 114)

2 onions, sliced

4 chicken legs

100ml (3½fl oz) dry white wine, water or stock

1 tbsp vegetable oil

new potatoes to serve

Chicken with Peperonata Sauce

For the peperonata sauce

2 large red peppers, halved and seeded

2 large yellow peppers, halved and seeded

1 tbsp extra virgin olive oil

1 fat garlic clove, roughly chopped

1 Preheat the oven to 200°C (180°C fan oven) mark 6. Spread the onions over the base of a large roasting tin. Put the chicken legs on top, then pour over 50ml (2fl oz) of the wine, water or stock. Roast the chicken for 15 minutes, then brush with the oil to crisp up the skin. Pour over remaining wine if the onions are browning too quickly. Roast for a further 25 minutes.

2 Meanwhile, make the peperonata sauce. Using a swivel-headed peeler, peel the peppers as thoroughly as you can. Apply as little pressure as possible, so you don't take off too much flesh under the skin. Cut the peppers into thin strips and put them in a frying pan with the olive oil. Cook over a medium heat for 5–7 minutes until they are just soft. Add the garlic for the last 2 minutes of cooking. Stir the peperonata sauce into the onions and cook for a further 5 minutes.

3 To serve, divide the chicken among four warm plates and serve with a spoonful of the pepper mixture and steamed new potatoes.

Serves 4	EASY		NUTRITIONAL INFORMATION	
	Preparation Time 20 minutes	**Cooking Time** 45 minutes	**Per Serving** 383 calories, 17g fat (of which 4g saturates), 20g carbohydrate. 0.4g salt	Gluten free • Dairy free

Cook's Tip

To enrich the flavour, add a splash of dry sherry or white wine to the pan when you add the rice.

Mushroom, Bacon and Leek Risotto

25g (1oz) dried mushrooms

250g (9oz) dry-cure smoked bacon, rind removed, chopped

3 leeks, chopped

300g (11oz) risotto rice

20g (³/₄oz) chives, chopped

25g (1oz) freshly grated Parmesan plus extra to sprinkle

1 Put the mushrooms in a large heatproof bowl and pour over 1.4 litres (2½ pints) boiling water. Leave to soak for 10 minutes.

2 Meanwhile, fry the bacon and leeks in a large pan – no need to add oil – for 7–8 minutes until soft and golden.

3 Stir in the rice, cook for 1–2 minutes, then add the mushrooms and their soaking liquor. Cook at a gentle simmer, stirring occasionally, for 15–20 minutes until the rice is cooked and most of the liquid has been absorbed.

4 Stir in the chives and grated Parmesan, then sprinkle with extra Parmesan to serve.

EASY		NUTRITIONAL INFORMATION		Serves
Preparation Time 10 minutes	**Cooking Time** about 30 minutes	**Per Serving** 452 calories, 13g fat (of which 5g saturates), 62g carbohydrate, 2.6g salt	Gluten free	**4**

Cook's Tip

Chillies vary enormously in strength, from quite mild to blisteringly hot, depending on the type of chilli and its ripeness. Taste a small piece first to check it's not too hot for you.

Be extremely careful when handling chillies not to touch or rub your eyes with your fingers, as they will sting. Wash knives immediately after handling chillies for the same reason. As a precaution, use rubber gloves when preparing them if you like.

Chilli Bolognese

1 tbsp olive oil

1 large onion, finely chopped

½ large red chilli, seeded and thinly sliced (see Cook's Tip)

450g (1lb) minced beef or lamb

125g (4oz) smoked bacon, rind removed, cut into strips

3 roasted red peppers, drained and finely chopped

400g can chopped tomatoes

125ml (4fl oz) red wine

300g (11oz) spaghetti

25g (1oz) freshly grated Cheddar or Gruyère cheese

2 tbsp freshly chopped flat-leafed parsley (optional)

salt and ground black pepper

1 Heat the oil in a large pan over a medium heat. Add the onion and chilli, and fry for 5–10 minutes until soft and golden. Add the beef or lamb and bacon, and stir over the heat for 5–7 minutes until well browned.

2 Stir in the red peppers, tomatoes and wine. Season, bring to the boil, then simmer over a low heat for 15–20 minutes.

3 Meanwhile, cook the spaghetti according to the packet instructions, then drain.

4 Just before serving, stir the grated cheese, parsley, if using, and the sauce into the spaghetti.

Serves 4	EASY		NUTRITIONAL INFORMATION
	Preparation Time 15 minutes	**Cooking Time** 30–40 minutes	**Per Serving** 756 calories, 33g fat (of which 13g saturates), 74g carbohydrate, 1.4g salt

Cook's Tip

If you can't find Desiree potatoes, use Maris Piper or King Edward instead.

Sausages with Roasted Onions and Potatoes

900g (2lb) Desiree potatoes, cut into wedges

4 tbsp olive oil

3–4 fresh rosemary sprigs (optional)

2 red onions, each cut into 8 wedges

8 sausages

salt and ground black pepper

1 Preheat the oven to 220°C (200°C fan oven) mark 7. Put the potatoes in the roasting tin – they should sit in one layer. Drizzle over the oil and season with salt and pepper. Toss well to coat the potatoes in oil, then put the rosemary on top, if using, and roast in the oven for 20 minutes.

2 Remove the roasting tin from the oven and add the onion wedges. Toss again to coat the onions and turn the potatoes. Put the sausages in between the potatoes and onions. Return the tin to the oven for 1 hour.

3 Divide among four plates and serve immediately.

EASY		NUTRITIONAL INFORMATION		Serves
Preparation Time 10 minutes	**Cooking Time** 1 hour 20 minutes	**Per Serving** 640 calories, 40g fat (of which 12g saturates), 55g carbohydrate, 2.5g salt	Dairy free	**4**

Cheesy Polenta with Tomato Sauce

oil to grease

225g (8oz) polenta

4 tbsp freshly chopped herbs, such as oregano, chives and flat-leafed parsley

100g (3½oz) freshly grated Parmesan

salt and ground black pepper

fresh Parmesan shavings to serve

For the tomato and basil sauce

1 tbsp vegetable oil

3 garlic cloves, crushed

500g carton creamed tomatoes or passata

1 bay leaf

1 fresh thyme sprig

caster sugar

3 tbsp freshly chopped basil, plus extra to garnish

1 Lightly oil a 25.5 x 18cm (10 x 7in) dish. In a large pan, bring 1.1 litres (2 pints) water and ¼ tsp salt to the boil. Sprinkle in the polenta, whisking constantly. Reduce the heat and simmer, stirring frequently, for 10–15 minutes until the mixture leaves the sides of the pan.

2 Stir in the herbs and Parmesan, and season to taste with salt and pepper. Turn into the prepared dish and leave to cool.

3 Next, make the tomato and basil sauce. Heat the oil in a pan and fry the garlic for 30 seconds (do not brown). Add the creamed tomatoes or passata, the bay leaf, thyme and a large pinch of sugar. Season with salt and pepper, bring to the boil and simmer, uncovered, for 5–10 minutes. Remove the bay leaf and thyme sprig, and add the chopped basil.

4 To serve, cut the polenta into pieces and lightly brush with oil. Preheat a griddle and fry for 3–4 minutes on each side, or grill under a preheated grill for 7–8 minutes on each side. Serve with the tomato and basil sauce, fresh Parmesan shavings and chopped basil.

Get Ahead

Complete to the end of step 3. Cover and chill separately for up to two days.
To use Complete the recipe.

Serves	EASY		NUTRITIONAL INFORMATION	
6	**Preparation Time** 15 minutes, plus cooling	**Cooking Time** 45 minutes	**Per Serving** 249 calories, 9g fat (of which 4g saturates), 31g carbohydrate, 0.9g salt	Vegetarian Gluten free

4

Weekend Meals

Freezing tip

Prepare the recipe to the first baking, turn out on to a baking sheet and cool, then wrap separately, label and freeze for up to one month.
To use Complete the recipe. Cook the soufflés from frozen at 200°C (180°C fan oven) mark 6 for 25–30 minutes until golden.

Twice-baked Soufflés

50g (2oz) butter plus extra to grease
25g (1oz) ground almonds, lightly toasted
250g (9oz) cauliflower florets
150ml (¼ pint) milk
40g (1½oz) plain flour
75g (3oz) Cheddar cheese, finely grated
75g (3oz) Emmenthal cheese, finely grated
3 large eggs, separated
300ml (½ pint) double cream
1 tbsp grainy mustard
salt and ground black pepper
rocket leaves and cherry tomatoes drizzled with olive oil and balsamic vinegar to serve

1 Preheat the oven to 180°C (160°C fan oven) mark 4. Grease and baseline eight 150ml (¼ pint) ramekins with greaseproof paper. Dust with the almonds.

2 Cook the cauliflower in salted boiling water until tender. Drain, plunge into iced water and drain again. Blend with the milk until smooth. Melt the butter in a pan, add the flour and mix to a smooth paste. Stir in the cauliflower purée and bring to the boil. Cool a little. Beat in the cheeses and egg yolks. Season. Whisk the whites to a soft peak and fold in. Spoon the mixture into the ramekins, put into a roasting tin and fill halfway up the sides with hot water. Cook for 20–25 minutes until firm to the touch. Remove from the tin and cool completely. Run a knife around the edge of the soufflés and turn out on to a baking sheet. Preheat the oven to 200°C (180°C fan oven) mark 6. Bring the cream to the boil in a wide pan. Bubble until reduced by one-third. Add the mustard and season. Spoon a little cream over the soufflés and bake for 15–20 minutes until golden. Serve with rocket leaves and cherry tomatoes.

Serves 8	A LITTLE EFFORT		NUTRITIONAL INFORMATION	
	Preparation Time 20 minutes, plus cooling	**Cooking Time** 1¼ hours	**Per Serving** 377 calories, 34g fat (of which 20g saturates), 7g carbohydrate, 0.6g salt	Vegetarian

Freezing tip

Freeze at step 3 for up to one month.
To use Cook from frozen on an upturned Swiss roll tin at 200°C (180°C fan oven) mark 6 for 45 minutes.

Cook's Tip

Traditional Parmesan is not strictly vegetarian, as it contains calves' rennet. However, most supermarkets now stock a vegetarian version.

Classic Nut Roast

40g (1½oz) butter

1 onion, finely chopped

1 garlic clove, crushed

125g (4oz) fresh white breadcrumbs

zest and juice of ½ lemon

225g (8oz) mixed white nuts, such as Brazil nuts, macadamia nuts, pinenuts and almonds, ground in a food processor

75g (3oz) vegetarian sage Derby or Parmesan cheese, grated

125g (4oz) canned peeled chestnuts, roughly chopped

½ x 390g can artichoke hearts, roughly chopped

1 medium egg, lightly beaten

2 tsp each freshly chopped parsley, sage and thyme, plus extra fresh sprigs

salt and ground black pepper

steamed mixed vegetables to serve

1 Preheat the oven to 200°C (180°C fan oven) mark 6. Melt the butter in a pan and cook the onion and garlic for 5 minutes or until soft. Put into a large bowl and set aside to cool.

2 Add the breadcrumbs, lemon zest and juice, ground nuts, grated cheese, chestnuts and artichokes. Season generously and bind the mixture together with the beaten egg. Stir in the freshly chopped herbs.

3 Put the mixture on to a large buttered piece of foil and shape into a fat, tightly packed rough sausage. Scatter over the extra herb sprigs and wrap in the foil.

4 Cook on an upturned Swiss roll tin for 30–40 minutes, then unwrap the foil slightly and cook for a further 15 minutes until it turns golden. Cut into thick slices and serve with steamed vegetables.

EASY		NUTRITIONAL INFORMATION		Serves
Preparation Time 20 minutes, plus cooling	**Cooking Time** about 1 hour	**Per Serving** 386 calories, 28g fat (of which 6g saturates), 23g carbohydrate, 0.7g salt	Vegetarian	**8**

Mixed Mushroom Cannelloni

6 sheets fresh lasagne

3 tbsp olive oil

1 small onion, finely sliced

3 garlic cloves, sliced

20g pack fresh thyme, finely chopped

225g (8oz) chestnut or brown-cap mushrooms, roughly chopped

125g (4oz) flat-cap mushrooms, roughly chopped

2 x 125g goat's cheese logs, with rind

350g carton cheese sauce

salt and ground black pepper

green salad to serve

Cook's Tip

Fresh lasagne sheets wrapped around a filling are used here to make cannelloni, but you can also buy dried cannelloni tubes, which can easily be filled using a teaspoon.

1 Preheat the oven to 180°C (160°C fan oven) mark 4. Cook the lasagne in boiling water until just tender. Drain well and run under cold water to cool. Keep covered with cold water until ready to use.

2 Heat the oil in a large pan and add the onion. Cook over a medium heat for 7–10 minutes until the onion is soft. Add the garlic and fry for 1–2 minutes. Keep a few slices of garlic to one side. Keep a little thyme for sprinkling over later, then add the rest to the pan with the mushrooms. Cook for a further 5 minutes or until the mushrooms are golden brown and there is no excess liquid in the pan. Season, remove from the heat and set aside.

3 Crumble one of the goat's cheese logs into the cooled mushroom mixture and stir together. Drain the lasagne sheets and pat dry with kitchen paper. Spoon 2–3 tbsp of the mushroom mixture along the long edge of each lasagne sheet, leaving a 1cm ($^1/_2$in) border. Roll up the pasta sheets and cut each roll in half. Put the pasta in a shallow ovenproof dish and spoon over the cheese sauce. Slice the remaining goat's cheese into thick rounds and arrange across the middle of the pasta rolls. Sprinkle the reserved garlic and thyme on top. Cook in the oven for 30–35 minutes until golden and bubbling. Serve with a green salad.

Serves 4	A LITTLE EFFORT		NUTRITIONAL INFORMATION	
	Preparation Time 15 minutes	**Cooking Time** 50–55 minutes	**Per Serving** 631 calories, 37g fat (of which 18g saturates), 50g carbohydrate, 1.9g salt	Vegetarian

Try Something Different

Mozzarella and tomato: spread the pizza bases with
4 tbsp pesto and top with 125g (4oz) chopped sunblush
tomatoes and 2 x 125g sliced mozzarella balls. Cook, then
serve topped with a handful of baby spinach leaves.
Ham and pineapple: spread the pizza bases with 4 tbsp
tomato pasta sauce. Top with a 225g can drained
unsweetened pineapple chunks, 125g (4oz) diced ham and
125g (4oz) grated Gruyère.

Tuna Melt Pizza

2 large pizza bases

4 tbsp sun-dried tomato pesto

2 x 185g cans tuna, drained

50g can anchovies, drained and chopped

125g (4oz) grated mature Cheddar cheese

rocket to serve

1 Preheat the oven to 220°C (200°C fan oven) mark 7.
Spread each pizza base with 2 tbsp sun-dried tomato
pesto. Top each with half the tuna, half the anchovies
and half the grated cheese.

2 Put on to a baking sheet and cook in the oven for
10–12 minutes until the cheese has melted. Sprinkle
with rocket to serve.

Serves 4	EASY		NUTRITIONAL INFORMATION
	Preparation Time 5 minutes	**Cooking Time** 10–12 minutes	**Per Serving** 688 calories, 26g fat (of which 9g saturates), 72g carbohydrate, 3.5g salt

Cook's Tips

Adding the stock gradually gives the risotto its deliciously creamy texture.

To make spring onion curls, thinly slice the onions lengthways, soak in ice-cold water for 30 minutes, then drain well.

Prawn and Lemon Risotto

225g (8oz) sugarsnap peas, sliced diagonally
175g (6oz) baby courgettes, sliced diagonally
2 tbsp olive oil
1 onion, finely chopped
¼ tsp saffron (optional)
225g (8oz) arborio (risotto) rice
1 garlic clove, crushed
225g (8oz) brown-cap mushrooms, quartered
zest and juice of 1 lemon
750ml (1¼ pints) hot fish, chicken or vegetable stock
300g (11oz) cooked peeled prawns
3 tbsp finely chopped chives
salt and ground black pepper
spring onion curls (see Cook's Tips) and grated lemon zest to garnish

1 Put the sugarsnap peas and courgettes in a large pan of boiling salted water, then bring to the boil. Cook for 1–2 minutes. Drain and plunge into ice-cold water.

2 Heat the oil in a medium non-stick pan, then add the onion and saffron, if using. Cook over a medium heat for 10 minutes or until soft. Add the rice, garlic and mushrooms, and cook, stirring, for 1–2 minutes. Season with salt and pepper.

3 Add the grated lemon zest and about one-third of the stock (see Cook's Tips). Simmer gently, stirring frequently, until most of the liquid has been absorbed. Add another one-third of the stock, then repeat the process.

4 Add the remaining stock. Cook, stirring, for 10 minutes or until the rice is tender and most of the stock has been absorbed. Add the prawns, drained vegetables, 1–2 tbsp lemon juice and the chives, then heat for 3–4 minutes. Garnish with spring onion curls and lemon zest.

EASY		NUTRITIONAL INFORMATION		Serves
Preparation Time 15 minutes	**Cooking Time** about 40 minutes	**Per Serving** 405 calories, 8g fat (of which 1g saturates), 59g carbohydrate, 0.9g salt	Gluten free • Dairy free	**4**

Try Something Different

Simple tartare sauce: mix 8 tbsp mayonnaise with 1 tbsp each chopped capers and gherkins, 1 tbsp freshly chopped tarragon or chives and 2 tsp lemon juice.
Herby lemon mayonnaise: fold 2 tbsp finely chopped parsley, grated zest of $\frac{1}{2}$ lemon and 2 tsp lemon juice into 8 tbsp mayonnaise.

Fish and Chips

900g (2lb) Desiree, Maris Piper or King Edward potatoes, peeled

2–3 tbsp olive oil

sea salt flakes

sunflower oil to deep-fry

2 x 128g packs batter mix

1 tsp baking powder

$\frac{1}{4}$ tsp salt

330ml bottle of lager

4 plaice fillets, about 225g (8oz) each, skin on, trimmed and cut in half

plain flour to dust

2 garlic cloves, crushed

8 tbsp mayonnaise

1 tsp lemon juice

salt and ground black pepper

lemon wedges and chives to garnish

1 Preheat the oven to 240°C (220°C fan oven) mark 9. Cut the potatoes into chips. Put them in a pan of boiling salted water, cover and bring to the boil. Boil for 2 minutes, drain well, then turn on to kitchen paper to remove the excess moisture. Tip into a large non-stick roasting tin, toss with the olive oil and season with sea salt. Roast for 40–50 minutes until golden and cooked, turning from time to time.

2 Meanwhile, half-fill a deep-fat fryer with sunflower oil and heat to 190°C. Put the batter mix into a bowl with the baking powder and salt, and gradually whisk in the lager. Season the plaice and lightly dust with flour. Dip two of the fillets into the batter and deep-fry in the hot oil until golden. Keep hot in the oven while you deep-fry the remaining plaice fillets.

3 Mix the garlic, mayonnaise and lemon juice together in a bowl and season well. Serve the garlic mayonnaise with the plaice and chips, garnished with lemon wedges and chives.

Serves	EASY		NUTRITIONAL INFORMATION	
4	**Preparation Time** 30 minutes	**Cooking Time** 40–50 minutes	**Per Serving** 993 calories, 67g fat (of which 9g saturates), 64g carbohydrate, 1.6g salt	Dairy free

2 medium baking potatoes, thinly sliced

a little freshly grated nutmeg

600ml (1 pint) white sauce (use a
ready-made sauce or make your own)

1/2 x 390g can fried onions

250g (9oz) frozen peas

450g (1lb) cooked chicken, shredded

20g pack garlic butter, sliced

a little butter to grease

salt and ground black pepper

steamed vegetables and
Granary bread (optional) to serve

Oven-baked Chicken with Garlic Potatoes

1 Preheat the oven to 180°C (160°C fan oven) mark 4.
Layer half the potatoes over the base of a 2.4 litre
(4¼ pint) shallow ovenproof dish and season with the
nutmeg, salt and pepper. Pour the white sauce over
and shake the dish, so that the sauce settles through
the gaps in the potatoes.

2 Spread half the onions on top, then scatter over half
the peas. Arrange the shredded chicken on top, then
add the remaining peas and onions. Finish with the
remaining potato, arranged in an even layer, and dot
with garlic butter. Season with salt and pepper.

3 Cover tightly with buttered foil and cook for 1 hour.
Turn the heat up to 200°C (180°C fan oven) mark 6,
remove the foil and continue to cook for 20–30
minutes until the potatoes are golden and tender.
Serve with steamed vegetables and, if you like, some
Granary bread to mop up the juices.

EASY		NUTRITIONAL INFORMATION	Serves
Preparation Time 10 minutes	**Cooking Time** 1½ hours	**Per Serving** 376 calories, 16g fat (of which 5g saturates), 32g carbohydrate, 1.2g salt	**6**

> **Weekend meal menu**

▼ Perfect Roast Chicken
▶ Instant Banana Ice Cream (see page 118)

Perfect Roast Chicken

1.8kg (4lb) free-range chicken
25g (1oz) butter, softened
2 tbsp olive oil
1 lemon, cut in half
1 small head of garlic, cut in half horizontally
salt and ground black pepper
new potatoes and seasonal vegetables such as green beans or mangetouts to serve

1 Preheat the oven to 220°C (200°C fan oven) mark 7. Put the chicken in a roasting tin just large enough to hold it comfortably. Spread the butter all over the chicken, then drizzle with the oil and season with salt and pepper.

2 Squeeze the lemon juice over it, then put one lemon half inside the chicken. Put the other half and the garlic into the roasting tin.

3 Put the chicken into the oven for 15 minutes then turn the heat down to 190°C (170°C fan oven) mark 5 and cook for a further 45 minutes–1 hour until the leg juices run clear when pierced with a skewer or sharp knife. While the bird is cooking, baste from time to time with the pan juices. Add a splash of water to the tin if the juices dry out.

4 Take the chicken out, put on a warm plate and cover with foil. Leave for 10 minutes before carving, so the juices that have risen to the surface soak back into the meat. This will make it more moist and easier to slice. Mash some of the garlic into the pan juices and serve the gravy with the chicken. Serve with new potatoes and seasonal vegetables.

EASY		NUTRITIONAL INFORMATION		Serves
Preparation Time 5 minutes	**Cooking Time** 1 hour–1¼ hours, plus resting	**Per Serving** 639 calories, 46g fat (of which 13g saturates), 0g carbohydrate, 0.6g salt	Gluten free	**4**

Weekend meal menu

▼ **Chicken Curry with Rice**

▶ **Exotic Fruit Salad** (see page 110)

Chicken Curry with Rice

2 tbsp vegetable oil

1 onion, finely sliced

2 garlic cloves, crushed

6 skinless chicken thigh fillets, cut into strips

2 tbsp tikka masala curry paste

200g can chopped tomatoes

450ml (¾ pint) hot vegetable stock

200g (7oz) basmati rice

1 tsp salt

225g (8oz) baby leaf spinach

poppadums and mango chutney to serve

1 Heat the oil in a large pan, add the onion and fry over a medium heat for about 5 minutes until golden. Add the garlic and chicken, and stir-fry for about 5 minutes until golden.

2 Add the curry paste, tomatoes and stock. Stir and bring to the boil, then cover with a lid and simmer on a low heat for 15 minutes or until the chicken is cooked (cut a piece in half to check that it's white all the way through).

3 Meanwhile, cook the rice. Put 600ml (1 pint) water in a medium pan, cover and bring to the boil. Add the rice and salt, and stir. Replace the lid and turn down the heat to its lowest setting. Cook for the time stated on the pack. Once cooked, cover with a teatowel and the lid. Leave for 5 minutes to absorb the steam.

4 Add the spinach to the curry and cook until just wilted.

5 Spoon the rice into bowls, add the curry and serve with poppadums and mango chutney.

Serves 4	EASY		NUTRITIONAL INFORMATION	
	Preparation Time 20 minutes	**Cooking Time** 25 minutes, plus 5 minutes standing	**Per Serving** 453 calories, 12g fat (of which 2g saturates), 49g carbohydrate, 2.4g salt	Gluten free • Dairy free

Marinated Pork with Vegetable Rice

1 tsp grated fresh root ginger

2 tbsp soy sauce

2 tbsp chopped rosemary

4 rindless pork steaks

150g (5oz) brown rice

450ml (¾ pint) hot vegetable stock

1 tbsp, plus 1 tsp olive oil

1 red onion, chopped

1 red pepper, chopped

a handful of shredded Savoy cabbage

1 Mix the grated root ginger, soy sauce and chopped rosemary in a shallow dish. Add the pork steaks, turn to coat, then set aside.

2 Put the rice in a pan and pour over the vegetable stock. Cover, bring to the boil, then simmer over a low heat for 20 minutes or until the rice is tender and the liquid has been absorbed.

3 Meanwhile, heat 1 tbsp olive oil in a frying pan. Add the red onion, red pepper and shredded cabbage. Fry for 10 minutes. Heat 1 tsp oil in a separate frying pan and fry the steaks for 4–5 minutes on each side. Stir the vegetables through the rice, then serve with the pork.

Serves 4	EASY		NUTRITIONAL INFORMATION	
	Preparation Time 10 minutes	**Cooking Time** 20 minutes	**Per Serving** 462 calories, 11g fat (of which 4g saturates), 41g carbohydrate, 2.2g salt	Gluten free • Dairy free

Cook's Tip

Put the hotpot under the grill for 2–3 minutes to crisp up the potatoes, if you like.

Freezing tip

Cool quickly, then freeze in the casserole for up to three months.
To use Thaw overnight at cool room temperature. Preheat the oven to 180°C (160°C fan oven) mark 4. Pour 50ml (2fl oz) hot stock over the hotpot, then cover and reheat for 30 minutes or until piping hot. Uncover and crisp the potatoes under the grill for 2–3 minutes.

Pork and Apple Hotpot

1 tbsp olive oil

900g (2lb) pork shoulder steaks

3 onions, cut into wedges

1 large Bramley apple, peeled, cored and thickly sliced

1 tbsp plain flour

600ml (1 pint) hot, weak chicken or vegetable stock

¼ Savoy cabbage, sliced

2 fresh thyme sprigs

900g (2lb) large potatoes, cut into 2cm (¾ in) slices

25g (1oz) butter

salt and ground black pepper

1 Preheat the oven to 170°C (150°C fan oven) mark 3. In a large, non-stick, flameproof and freezerproof casserole, heat the oil until very hot, then fry the steaks, two at a time, for 5 minutes or until golden all over. Remove the steaks from the pan and set aside.

2 In the same casserole, fry the onions for 10 minutes or until soft – add a little water if they start to stick. Stir in the apple and cook for 1 minute, then add the flour to soak up the juices. Gradually add the stock and stir until smooth. Season. Stir in the cabbage and add the pork.

3 Throw in the thyme, overlap the potato slices on top, then dot with the butter. Cover with a tight-fitting lid and cook near the top of the oven for 1 hour. Remove the lid and cook for 30–45 minutes until the potatoes are tender and golden.

EASY		NUTRITIONAL INFORMATION	Serves
Preparation Time 15 minutes	**Cooking Time** 2–2¼ hours	**Per Serving** 592 calories, 18g fat (of which 7g saturates), 56g carbohydrate, 1g salt	**4**

Weekend meal menu

▼ Roasted Venison Sausages
▶ Baked Orange Custard (see page 117)

Roasted Venison Sausages

12 venison sausages
2 tbsp redcurrant jelly
1 tsp lemon juice

For the red onion marmalade

400g (14oz) red onions, chopped
2 tbsp olive oil
4 tbsp red wine vinegar
2 tbsp demerara sugar
1 tsp juniper berries, crushed
mashed potatoes to serve

1 Preheat the oven to 220°C (200°C fan oven) mark 7. Put the sausages into a small roasting tin. Mix together the redcurrant jelly and lemon juice and spoon over the sausages. Roast for 35 minutes, turning once.

2 Meanwhile, make the red onion marmalade. Gently fry the onions in the oil for 15–20 minutes. Add the vinegar, sugar and juniper berries, and continue cooking for 5 minutes or until the onions are really tender.

3 Serve the sausages with the red onion marmalade and mashed potatoes.

Serves 6	EASY		NUTRITIONAL INFORMATION	
	Preparation Time 10 minutes	**Cooking Time** 35 minutes	**Per Serving** 439 calories, 32g fat (of which 12g saturates), 28g carbohydrate, 2.4g salt	Dairy free

Try Something Different

Add a handful of shredded spinach with the mint.

Lamb with Orange and Mint

4 tbsp olive oil

4 lamb steaks, about 700g (1½lb) total weight

185g jar chargrilled sweet red peppers, drained and roughly chopped

50g (2oz) black olives

1 orange

juice of 1 lemon

1 small bunch mint, roughly chopped

salt and ground black pepper

1 Heat 2 tbsp oil in a large non-stick frying pan. Brown the lamb in the hot oil, turning occasionally until the meat has formed a deep golden-brown crust all over.

2 Lower the heat and add the peppers and olives to the pan. Chop up the orange, squeeze the juice directly into the pan and add the orange pieces for extra flavour. Add the lemon juice and the remaining oil.

3 Simmer for 5 minutes, stirring to break down the peppers a little. Stir the mint into the pan. Season to taste with salt and pepper and serve.

EASY		NUTRITIONAL INFORMATION		Serves
Preparation Time 10 minutes	**Cooking Time** 20 minutes	**Per Serving** 451 calories, 32g fat (of which 11g saturates), 6g carbohydrate, 1.1g salt	Gluten free • Dairy free	**4**

Greek Lamb and Feta Layer

5 tbsp olive oil

1 large onion, finely chopped

900g (2lb) lamb mince

2 garlic cloves, crushed

2 tbsp tomato purée

2 x 400g cans plum tomatoes in tomato juice

3 tbsp Worcestershire sauce

2 tbsp freshly chopped oregano

3 large potatoes, about 1kg (2¼lb) total weight

2 large aubergines, trimmed and cut into 5mm (¼ in) slices

1kg (2¼ lb) Greek yogurt

4 large eggs

50g (2oz) freshly grated Parmesan

pinch of freshly grated nutmeg

200g (7oz) feta cheese, crumbled

salt and ground black pepper

1 Heat 2 tbsp oil in a large pan, add the onion and cook over a low heat for 10 minutes or until soft. Put the mince in a large non-stick frying pan and cook over a high heat, breaking it up with a spoon, until no liquid remains and the lamb is brown, 10–15 minutes. Add the garlic and tomato purée, and cook for 2 minutes. Add the lamb to the onion with the tomatoes, Worcestershire sauce and oregano. Bring to the boil and season with salt and pepper. Simmer for 30–40 minutes until the lamb is tender.

2 Meanwhile, cook the potatoes in boiling salted water for 20–30 minutes until tender, then drain and cool. Peel and slice thickly. Preheat the oven to 180°C (160°C fan oven) mark 4. Brush the aubergine slices with the remaining oil. Preheat two non-stick frying pans and cook the aubergine slices for 2–3 minutes on each side until soft. Mix together the yogurt, eggs and half the Parmesan, season the sauce to taste with salt and pepper, then add the nutmeg.

3 Divide the lamb between two 1.4 litre (2½ pint) ovenproof dishes or eight individual dishes. Layer the potato, feta and aubergine on top. Pour the yogurt sauce over and sprinkle with the remaining Parmesan. Cook for 35–40 minutes until the top has browned and it's piping hot in the centre.

Freezing tip

When you have layered the lamb, vegetables, feta, yogurt sauce and Parmesan in the dishes at step 3, cool, wrap and freeze for up to three months.
To use Thaw overnight at cool room temperature. Cook at 190°C (170°C fan oven) mark 5 for 45–50 minutes until piping hot in the centre.

A LITTLE EFFORT		NUTRITIONAL INFORMATION		Serves
Preparation Time 20 minutes	**Cooking Time** about 1 hour 50 minutes	**Per Serving** 684 calories, 45g fat (of which 20g saturates), 32g carbohydrate, 1.8g salt	Gluten free	**8**

Steak and Chips

2 large potatoes, peeled and cut into chips

2 tbsp olive oil

4 sirloin steaks, 125g (4oz) each, fat trimmed

25g (1oz) Roquefort cheese, cut into four small pieces

salt and ground black pepper

watercress to garnish

1 Preheat the oven to 220°C (200°C fan oven) mark 7. Put the potato chips into a pan of lightly salted water. Bring to the boil, then simmer for 4–5 minutes. Drain well.

2 Put the chips into a roasting tin, toss with 1 tbsp olive oil and cook in the oven, turning once, for 30–40 minutes or until cooked through and golden.

3 When the chips are nearly done, heat a non-stick frying pan until really hot. Brush the remaining oil over the steaks and season with salt and pepper. Add to the pan and fry for 2–3 minutes on each side for medium rare, or 2 minutes more if you prefer the meat well done. Put on to warmed plates, top each steak with a small piece of Roquefort while still hot and serve with the chips. Garnish with watercress.

Serves 4	EASY		NUTRITIONAL INFORMATION	
	Preparation Time 10 minutes	**Cooking Time** 35–45 minutes	**Per Serving** 318 calories, 13g fat (of which 5g saturates), 18g carbohydrate, 0.4g salt	Gluten free

Weekend meal menu

▼ Roast Beef with Tomato and Basil Sauce
▶ Raspberry Meringue Pie (see page 126)

Roast Beef with Tomato and Basil Sauce

800g (1lb 12oz) beef fillet
2 tbsp olive oil
1 red onion, finely sliced
300g (11oz) cherry tomatoes, halved
1 tbsp red wine vinegar
100ml (3½ fl oz) hot beef or vegetable stock
small handful of basil leaves, roughly torn if large
salt and ground black pepper
couscous to serve

1 Preheat the oven to 200°C (180°C fan oven) mark 6. Season the beef with salt and pepper. Heat 1 tbsp olive oil in a large frying pan and fry the beef for 5 minutes, turning, until browned on all sides. Put into a roasting tin and roast for 20–30 minutes – it should still be pink in the middle.

2 Meanwhile, add the remaining oil to the pan in which you fried the beef. Add the red onion and cook for 5–10 minutes over a medium heat until softened and golden. Add the tomatoes and continue to cook for 5 minutes until they're starting to soften.

3 Add the vinegar and stock, and bring to the boil. Bubble for 1–2 minutes, then add the basil. Taste and adjust the seasoning.

4 Cover the meat in kitchen foil and allow to rest for 10 minutes. Slice and serve with the sauce and couscous.

EASY		NUTRITIONAL INFORMATION		Serves
Preparation Time 10 minutes	**Cooking Time** 35 minutes	**Per Serving** 430 calories, 25g fat (of which 9g saturates), 6g carbohydrate, 0.8g salt	Gluten free • Dairy free	**4**

5

Perfect Puddings

Exotic Fruit Salad

1 pineapple, about 900g (2lb), peeled, cored
and cut into chunks

2 papayas, peeled, seeded and sliced

1 Galia melon, seeded, and flesh cut into chunks

fresh mint leaves to decorate

For the syrup

125g (4oz) caster sugar

6 fresh mint sprigs

$1/_4$ tsp Chinese five-spice powder

2 small fresh bay leaves

4 lemongrass stalks, split in half and bruised

$1/_2$ tsp grated fresh root ginger

1 To make the syrup, put the sugar in a pan with 600ml (1 pint) water and the remaining syrup ingredients. Heat gently until the sugar has dissolved. Bring to the boil and simmer for 5 minutes. Remove from the heat and set aside to infuse for at least 1 hour.

2 Put all the fruit in a bowl, strain the cooled syrup over the top, then cover and chill for at least 2 hours. Decorate with mint leaves.

	EASY		**NUTRITIONAL INFORMATION**	
Serves 6	**Preparation Time** 30 minutes, plus 3 hours infusing and chilling	**Cooking Time** 7 minutes	**Per Serving** 232 calories, 1g fat (of which 0g saturates), 58g carbohydrate, 0.1g salt	Vegetarian Gluten free • Dairy free

Get ahead

Complete step 1 to end of line 5 and spoon the dip into a bowl. Cover and chill for up to two days. Thread the fruit on to the skewers as in step 2. Cover and chill for up to one day.
To use Drizzle the dip with honey, sprinkle with toasted nuts and dust with cinnamon. Allow the chilled kebabs to come to room temperature. Finally, complete step 2.

Fruit Kebabs with Spiced Pear Dip

3 large fresh figs, cut into quarters

1 large ripe mango, peeled, stoned and cut into cubes

1 baby pineapple or 2 thick slices, peeled and cut into cubes

1 tbsp clear honey

For the spiced pear dip

150g (5oz) ready-to-eat dried pears, soaked in hot water for about 30 minutes

juice of 1 orange

1 tsp finely chopped fresh root ginger

$\frac{1}{2}$ tsp vanilla extract

50g (2oz) very low-fat plain yogurt

$\frac{1}{2}$ tsp ground cinnamon, plus extra to dust

1 tsp clear honey

25g (1oz) hazelnuts, toasted and roughly chopped

1 Soak six 20.5cm (8in) wooden skewers in water for 30 minutes. To make the dip, drain the pears and put in a food processor or blender with the orange juice, ginger, vanilla extract, yogurt, cinnamon and 50ml (2fl oz) water, and whiz until smooth. Spoon the dip into a bowl. Drizzle with the honey, sprinkle with the toasted hazelnuts and dust with a little ground cinnamon. Cover and set aside in a cool place until ready to serve.

2 Preheat the grill to its highest setting. To make the kebabs, thread pieces of fruit on to the skewers, using at least two pieces of each type of fruit per skewer. Put the skewers on a foil-covered tray. Drizzle with honey and grill for about 4 minutes on each side, close to the heat, until lightly charred. Serve warm or at room temperature with the spiced pear dip.

EASY		NUTRITIONAL INFORMATION		Serves
Preparation Time 20 minutes, plus 30 minutes soaking	**Cooking Time** 8 minutes	**Per Serving** 122 calories, 3g fat (of which trace saturates), 23g carbohydrate, 0g salt	Vegetarian Gluten free	**6**

Cook's Tips

Gelatine is available in leaf and powdered forms. Both must be soaked in liquid to soften before being dissolved in a warm liquid. Always add dissolved gelatine to a mixture that is warm or at room temperature – if added to a cold liquid, it will set in fine threads and spoil the final texture of the dish.

Gelatine is derived from meat bones, but there are also several vegetarian alternatives, such as agar agar and gelazone.

Elderflower and Fruit Jelly

2–3 tbsp elderflower cordial

200g (7oz) caster sugar

4 gelatine leaves

150g (5oz) raspberries

150g (5oz) seedless grapes, halved

1 Put the elderflower cordial into a large pan and add 750ml (1¼ pints) water and the sugar. Heat gently, stirring to dissolve the sugar.

2 Soak the gelatine leaves in cold water for 5 minutes. Lift out the gelatine, squeeze out the excess water, then add to the liquid in the pan. Stir to dissolve, then strain into a jug.

3 Divide the raspberries and grapes among six 200ml (7fl oz) glass dishes. Pour the liquid over the fruit, then cool and chill for at least 4 hours or overnight.

Serves 6	EASY		NUTRITIONAL INFORMATION	
	Preparation Time 15 minutes, plus min 4 hours chilling	**Cooking Time** 10 minutes	**Per Serving** 189 calories, 0g fat, 42g carbohydrate, 0g salt	Gluten free • Dairy free

Cook's Tip

Using a good-quality lemon curd will make all the difference to the final flavour of this fool.

Lemon and Passion Fruit Fool

6 tbsp lemon curd

4 ripe passion fruits

150ml (¼ pint) double cream

1 tbsp icing sugar

200g (7oz) Greek yogurt

toasted flaked almonds to decorate

1 Put the lemon curd into a small bowl. Halve the passion fruit and spoon the pulp into a sieve resting over a bowl. Stir to separate the seeds from the juice. Add 1 tbsp of the passion fruit juice to the lemon curd and mix well.

2 In a large bowl, whip the cream with the icing sugar until soft peaks form. Stir in the yogurt.

3 Put a dollop of yogurt cream into each of six small glasses. Layer with a spoonful of lemon curd mixture and 1 tsp passion fruit juice. Repeat to use up all the ingredients. Scatter over some toasted flaked almonds and serve immediately.

EASY	NUTRITIONAL INFORMATION		Serves
Preparation Time 20 minutes	**Per Serving** 210 calories, 17g fat (of which 10g saturates), 14g carbohydrate, 0.1g salt	Vegetarian Gluten free	**6**

Apples with Butterscotch Sauce

125g (4oz) sultanas

2 tbsp brandy

6 large Bramley apples, cored

4 tbsp soft brown sugar

2 tbsp apple juice

125g (4oz) hazelnuts, chopped and toasted

ricotta cheese to serve

For the butterscotch sauce

125g (4oz) butter

125g (4oz) soft brown sugar

2 tbsp golden syrup

2 tbsp black treacle

4 tbsp brandy

300ml (½ pint) double cream

1 Soak the sultanas in the brandy and set aside for 10 minutes, then stuff each apple with equal amounts.

2 Preheat the oven to 220°C (200°C fan oven) mark 7. Put the apples in a roasting tin, sprinkle over the brown sugar and apple juice. Bake for 15–20 minutes until soft.

3 Meanwhile, make the sauce. Melt the butter, brown sugar, golden syrup and treacle in a heavy-based pan, stirring continuously. When the sugar has dissolved and the mixture is bubbling, stir in the brandy and cream. Bring back to the boil and set aside.

4 Remove the apples from the oven. Serve the apples with the butterscotch sauce, hazelnuts and a dollop of ricotta cheese.

Get ahead

Complete step 1 up to 4 hours in advance.
Make the sauce (step 3), then cool, cover and chill for up to one day.
To use Complete the recipe and bring the sauce back to the boil to serve.

Serves	EASY		NUTRITIONAL INFORMATION	
6	**Preparation Time** 5 minutes, plus 10 minutes soaking	**Cooking Time** 15–20 minutes	**Per Serving** 821 calories, 56g fat (of which 28g saturates), 70g carbohydrate, 0.4g salt	Vegetarian Gluten free

Strawberry Compote

175g (6oz) raspberry conserve
juice of 1 orange
juice of 1 lemon
1 tsp rosewater
350g (12oz) strawberries, hulled and thickly sliced
150g (5oz) blueberries

1 Put the raspberry conserve into a pan with the orange and lemon juices. Add 75ml (2½ fl oz) boiling water. Stir over a low heat to melt the conserve, then leave to cool.

2 Stir in the rosewater and taste – you may want to add a squeeze more lemon juice if it's too sweet. Put the strawberries and blueberries into a large serving bowl. Strain over the raspberry conserve mixture. Cover and chill overnight. Remove the bowl from the refrigerator about 30 minutes before serving.

Serves	EASY		NUTRITIONAL INFORMATION	
4	Preparation Time 15 minutes, plus overnight chilling	Cooking Time 10 minutes	Per Serving 156 calories, 0g fat, 40g carbohydrate, 0g salt	Vegetarian Gluten free • Dairy free

Cook's Tips

Look for a mild flower honey such as lavender or orange blossom; a strong honey will be overpowering.
The honey needs to be cooked to a golden-brown caramel – any darker and it will become bitter.
The custard may still be wobbly after cooking, but don't worry, it firms up on cooling and chilling.

Baked Orange Custard

zest of 1 orange
450ml (³/₄ pint) milk
150ml (¹/₄ pint) double cream
75g (3oz) clear honey (see Cook's Tips)
2 large eggs, plus 4 large yolks
25g (1oz) caster sugar
slivers of orange zest to decorate

1 Put the orange zest, milk and cream in a pan, then bring to the boil. Set aside for 30 minutes to infuse.

2 Preheat the oven to 150°C (130°C fan oven) mark 2. Warm a 1.7 litre (3 pint) soufflé dish or six 150ml (¹/₄ pint) coffee cups in the oven. Bring the honey to the boil in a small heavy-based pan. Bubble for 2–3 minutes until it begins to caramelise (see Cook's Tips). Pour the caramel into the warmed dish or cups and rotate to coat the base. Set aside to cool and harden.

3 Put the eggs, yolks and sugar into a bowl and beat together until smooth. Add the infused milk mixture, stir until well combined, then strain into the dish(es). Put the dish or cups in a roasting tin, adding enough hot water to come halfway up the side(s). Bake for 1 hour 10 minutes for the soufflé dish or 45–50 minutes for the coffee cups until just set in the middle (see Cook's Tips). Cool and chill for at least 6 hours or overnight. Decorate with orange zest.

EASY		NUTRITIONAL INFORMATION		Serves
Preparation Time 10 minutes, plus 30 minutes infusing and 15 minutes cooling	**Cooking Time** 50 minutes or 1 hour 10 minutes, plus minimum 6 hours chilling	**Per Serving** 268 calories, 20g fat (of which 10g saturates), 18g carbohydrate, 0.2g salt	Vegetarian Gluten free	**6**

Cook's Tip

To freeze bananas, peel and slice them thinly, then put the banana slices on a large non-stick baking tray and put into the freezer for 30 minutes or until frozen. Transfer to a plastic bag and store in the freezer until needed.

6 ripe bananas, about 700g (1½lb), peeled, cut into thin slices and frozen (see Cook's Tip)

1–2 tbsp virtually fat-free fromage frais

1–2 tbsp orange juice

1 tsp vanilla extract

splash of rum or Cointreau (optional)

a few drops of lime juice to taste

Instant Banana Ice Cream

1 Leave the frozen banana slices to stand at room temperature for 2–3 minutes. Put the still frozen pieces in a food processor or blender with 1 tbsp fromage frais, 1 tbsp orange juice, the vanilla extract and the liqueur, if using.

2 Whiz until smooth, scraping down the sides of the bowl and adding more fromage frais and orange juice as necessary to give a creamy consistency. Add lime juice to taste and serve at once or turn into a freezer container and freeze for up to one month.

Serves 4	EASY		NUTRITIONAL INFORMATION	
	Preparation Time 5 minutes, plus 30 minutes freezing		**Per Serving** 173 calories, 1g fat (of which 0g saturates), 42g carbohydrate, 0g salt	Vegetarian Gluten free

Try Something Different

Although wild lingonberry sauce is used here, a spoonful of any fruit sauce or compote such as strawberry or blueberry will taste delicious.
For an alternative presentation, serve in tumblers, layering the rice pudding with the fruit sauce; you will need to use double the amount of fruit sauce.

Fruity Rice Pudding

125g (4oz) pudding rice
1.1 litres (2 pints) full-fat milk
1 tsp vanilla extract
3–4 tbsp caster sugar
200ml (7fl oz) whipping cream
6 tbsp wild lingonberry sauce

1 Put the rice in a pan with 600ml (1 pint) cold water, bring to the boil and simmer until the liquid has evaporated. Add the milk, bring to the boil and simmer for 45 minutes or until the rice is very soft and creamy. Leave to cool.

2 Add the vanilla extract and sugar to the rice. Lightly whip the cream and fold through the pudding. Chill for 1 hour.

3 Divide the rice mixture among six glass dishes and top with 1 tbsp lingonberry sauce.

EASY		NUTRITIONAL INFORMATION		Serves
Preparation Time 10 minutes, plus 30 minutes cooling and minimum 1 hour chilling	**Cooking Time** 1 hour	**Per Serving** 323 calories, 17g fat (of which 10g saturates), 36g carbohydrate, 0.2g salt	Vegetarian Gluten free	**6**

Toffee Cheesecake

300g (11oz) digestive biscuits, broken

125g (4oz) butter, melted

For the filling

450g (1lb) curd cheese

150ml (¼ pint) double cream

juice of ½ lemon

3 medium eggs, beaten

50g (2oz) golden caster sugar

6 tbsp dulce de leche toffee sauce, plus extra to drizzle

Cook's Tip

To slice the cheesecake easily, use a sharp knife dipped into a jug of boiling water and then wiped dry.

1 Preheat the oven to 200°C (180°C fan oven) mark 6. To make the crust, put the biscuits into a food processor and grind until fine. (Alternatively, put them in a plastic bag and crush with a rolling pin. Transfer to a bowl.) Add the butter and blend briefly, or stir in, to combine. Press the mixture evenly into the base and up the sides of a 20.5cm (8in) springform cake tin. Chill in the refrigerator.

2 To make the filling, put the curd cheese and cream in a food processor or blender and blend until smooth. Add the lemon juice, eggs, sugar and toffee sauce, then blend again until smooth. Pour into the chilled biscuit case and bake for 10 minutes. Reduce the oven temperature to 180°C (160°C fan oven) mark 4, then bake for 45 minutes or until set and golden brown.

3 Turn off the oven, leave the door ajar and let the cheesecake cool. When completely cool, chill to firm up the crust.

4 Remove the cheesecake from the tin by running a knife around the edge. Open the tin carefully, then use a palette knife to ease the cheesecake out. Cut into wedges, put on a serving plate, then drizzle with toffee sauce.

EASY		NUTRITIONAL INFORMATION		Serves
Preparation Time 15 minutes, plus chilling	**Cooking Time** 55 minutes–1 hour	**Per Serving** 439 calories, 32g fat (of which 19g saturates), 29g carbohydrate, 1.2g salt	Vegetarian	**10**

Try Something Different

Serve with sliced bananas and vanilla ice cream instead of the fruit compote and yogurt.

Cinnamon Pancakes

150g (5oz) plain flour

½ tsp ground cinnamon

1 medium egg

300ml (½ pint) skimmed milk

olive oil to fry

fruit compote or sugar and Greek yogurt to serve

1 In a large bowl, whisk together the flour, cinnamon, egg and milk to make a smooth batter. Leave to stand for 20 minutes.

2 Heat a heavy-based frying pan over a medium heat. When the pan is really hot, add 1 tsp oil, pour in a ladleful of batter and tilt the pan to coat the base with an even layer. Cook for 1 minute or until golden. Flip over and cook for 1 minute. Repeat with the remaining batter, adding more oil if necessary, to make six pancakes. Serve with a fruit compote or a sprinkling of sugar, and a dollop of yogurt.

Serves 6	EASY		NUTRITIONAL INFORMATION	
	Preparation Time 5 minutes	**Cooking Time** 20 minutes	**Per Serving** 141 calories, 5g fat (of which 1g saturates), 20g carbohydrate, 0.1g salt	Vegetarian

450g (1lb) rhubarb, cut into 2.5cm (1in) pieces

2 ripe pears, peeled, cored and roughly chopped

75g (3oz) demerara sugar

1 tsp ground cinnamon

50g (2oz) butter, chilled

75g (3oz) self-raising flour

2 shortbread fingers

50g (2oz) hazelnuts

Greek yogurt to serve

Rhubarb and Pear Crumble

1 Preheat the oven to 180°C (160°C fan oven) mark 4. Put the fruit into a small shallow baking dish and sprinkle over 25g (1oz) sugar and the cinnamon. Mix together well.

2 Next, make the crumble mixture. Put the butter in a food processor, add the flour and the remaining sugar and whiz until it looks like rough breadcrumbs. Alternatively, rub the fat into the flour by hand or using a pastry cutter, then stir in the sugar.

3 Break the shortbread fingers into pieces and add to the processor with the hazelnuts, or crush the shortbread with a rolling pin and chop the hazelnuts. Whiz again for 4–5 seconds until the crumble is blended but still looks rough. Sprinkle the crumble over the fruit, spreading it up to the edges and pressing down with the back of a wooden spoon.

4 Bake for 40–45 minutes until the topping is golden brown and crisp. Serve with yogurt.

EASY		NUTRITIONAL INFORMATION		Serves
Preparation Time 25 minutes	**Cooking Time** 40–45 minutes	**Per Serving** 255 calories, 14g fat (of which 6g saturates), 32g carbohydrate, 0.2g salt	Vegetarian	**6**

Caramelised Orange Trifle

125g (4oz) light muscovado sugar
2 x 135g packs orange jelly, broken into cubes
100ml (3½fl oz) brandy
10 oranges, peeled and all pith removed
150g (5oz) ratafia biscuits
4 tbsp sweet sherry
500g carton fresh custard sauce
300ml (½ pint) double cream
2 x 250g cartons mascarpone cheese
¼ tsp vanilla extract
125g (4oz) granulated sugar

Try Something Different

For an alternative decoration, try sprinkling silver dragees, crystallised flowers, toasted flaked almonds or grated chocolate over instead of the sugar strands.

1 Put the muscovado sugar in a large heavy-based pan. Add 100ml (3½ fl oz) water and dissolve the sugar over a low heat. Increase the heat and cook for 5 minutes or until the sugar is syrupy and thick. Remove from the heat and add 450ml (¾ pint) boiling water (the sugar will splutter). Add the jelly and stir until dissolved. Add the brandy and set aside.

2 Slice the orange flesh into rounds, putting any juice to one side. Add the juice – about 125ml (4fl oz) – to the jelly. Cool. Tip the ratafia biscuits into the base of a 3.5 litre (6¼ pint) bowl and drizzle with sherry. Arrange the orange rounds on top, then pour the jelly over. Chill for 4 hours until set.

3 Pour the custard over the top and smooth over. Put the cream, mascarpone and vanilla extract in a bowl and combine with an electric hand mixer. Spoon three-quarters of the mixture on to the custard. Smooth the surface. Put the remainder in a piping bag and pipe 10 swirls around the edge. Chill.

4 Line a large baking sheet with baking parchment. Half-fill the sink with cold water. Heat the granulated sugar in a heavy-based pan until dissolved. Increase the heat and cook to a golden caramel, then plunge the base of the pan into the sink. Dip in a fork and pick up the caramel, then flick it back and forth over the parchment to form fine strands. Put the sugar strands on top of the trifle.

Serves 16	FOR THE CONFIDENT COOK		NUTRITIONAL INFORMATION
	Preparation Time 45 minutes, plus 5 hours chilling	**Cooking Time** 5 minutes	**Per Serving** 376 calories, 16g fat (of which 10g saturates), 50g carbohydrate, 0.2g salt

Try Something Different

Replace the raspberry liqueur with another fruit-based liqueur such as Grand Marnier.

Raspberry Meringue Pie

8 trifle sponges

450g (1lb) raspberries, lightly crushed

2–3 tbsp raspberry liqueur

3 medium egg whites

150g (5oz) golden caster sugar

1 Preheat the oven to 230°C (210°C fan oven) mark 8. Put the trifle sponges in the bottom of a 2 litre (3½ pint) ovenproof dish. Spread the raspberries on top and drizzle over the raspberry liqueur.

2 Whisk the egg whites in a clean grease-free bowl until stiff peaks form. Gradually whisk in the sugar until the mixture is smooth and glossy. Spoon the meringue mixture over the raspberries and bake for 6–8 minutes until golden.

Serves 8	EASY		NUTRITIONAL INFORMATION	
	Preparation Time 15 minutes	**Cooking Time** 6–8 minutes	**Per Serving** 252 calories, 3g fat (of which trace saturates), 49g carbohydrate, 0.2g salt	Vegetarian

Glossary

Al dente Italian term commonly used to describe food, especially pasta and vegetables, which are cooked until tender but still firm to the bite.

Baking blind Pre-baking a pastry case before filling. The pastry case is lined with greaseproof paper and weighted down with dried beans or ceramic baking beans.

Baste To spoon the juices and melted fat over meat, poultry, game or vegetables during roasting to keep them moist. The term is also used to describe spooning over a marinade.

Beat To incorporate air into an ingredient or mixture by agitating it vigorously with a spoon, fork, whisk or electric mixer. The technique is also used to soften ingredients.

Bind To mix beaten egg or other liquid into a dry mixture to hold it together.

Blanch To immerse food briefly in fast-boiling water to loosen skins, such as peaches or tomatoes, or to remove bitterness, or to destroy enzymes and preserve the colour, flavour and texture of vegetables (especially prior to freezing).

Bouquet garni Small bunch of herbs – usually a mixture of parsley stems, thyme and a bay leaf – tied in muslin and used to flavour stocks, soups and stews.

Braise To cook meat, poultry, game or vegetables slowly in a small amount of liquid in a pan or casserole with a tight-fitting lid. The food is usually first browned in oil or fat.

Caramelise To heat sugar or sugar syrup slowly until it is brown in colour; ie forms a caramel.

Chill To cool food in the fridge.

Compote Fresh or dried fruit stewed in sugar syrup. Served hot or cold.

Coulis A smooth fruit or vegetable purée, thinned if necessary to a pouring consistency.

Cream To beat together fat and sugar until the mixture is pale and fluffy, and resembles whipped cream in texture and colour. The method is used in cakes and puddings which contain a high proportion of fat and require the incorporation of a lot of air.

Croûtons Small pieces of fried or toasted bread, served with soups and salads.

Crudités Raw vegetables, usually cut into slices or sticks, typically served with a dipping sauce.

Curdle To cause sauces or creamed mixtures to separate, usually by overheating or over-beating.

Cure To preserve fish, meat or poultry by smoking, drying or salting.

Deglaze To heat stock, wine or other liquid with the cooking juices left in the pan after roasting or sautéeing, scraping and stirring vigorously to dissolve the sediment on the bottom of the pan.

Dice To cut food into small cubes.

Dredge To sprinkle food generously with flour, sugar, icing sugar etc.

Dust To sprinkle lightly with flour, cornflour, icing sugar etc.

Escalope Thin slice of meat, such as pork, veal or turkey, from the top of the leg, usually pan-fried.

Fillet Term used to describe boned breasts of birds, boned sides of fish, and the undercut of a loin of beef, lamb, pork or veal.

Flake To separate food, such as cooked fish, into natural pieces.

Folding in Method of combining a whisked or creamed mixture with other ingredients by cutting and folding so that it retains its lightness. A large metal spoon or plastic-bladed spatula is used.

Fry To cook food in hot fat or oil. There are various methods: shallow-frying in a little fat in a shallow pan; deep-frying where the food is totally immersed in oil; dry-frying in which fatty foods are cooked in a non-stick pan without extra fat; see also Stir-frying.

Garnish A decoration, usually edible, such as parsley or lemon, which is used to enhance the appearance of a savoury dish.

Gluten A protein constituent of grains, such as wheat and rye, which develops when the flour is missed with water to give the dough elasticity.

Griddle A flat, heavy, metal plate used on the hob for cooking scones or for searing savoury ingredients.

Gut To clean out the entrails from fish.

Hull To remove the stalk and calyx from soft fruits, such as strawberries.

Infuse To immerse flavourings, such as aromatic vegetables, herbs, spices and vanilla, in a liquid to impart flavour. Usually the infused liquid is brought to the boil, then left to stand for a while.

Julienne Fine 'matchstick' strips of vegetables or citrus zest, sometimes used as a garnish.

Macerate To soften and flavour raw or dried foods by soaking in a liquid, eg soaking fruit in alcohol.

Marinate To soak raw meat, poultry or game – usually in a mixture of oil, wine, vinegar and flavourings – to soften and impart flavour. The mixture, which is known as a marinade, may also be used to baste the food during cooking.

Medallion Small round piece of meat, usually beef or veal.

Mince To cut food into very fine pieces, using a mincer, food processor or knife.

Parboil To boil a vegetable or other food for part of its cooking time before finishing it by another method.

Pare To finely peel the skin or zest from vegetables or fruit.

Poach To cook food gently in liquid at simmering point; the surface should be just trembling.

Pot roast To cook meat in a covered pan with some fat and a little liquid.

Purée To pound, sieve or liquidise vegetables, fish or fruit to a smooth pulp. Purées often form the basis for soups and sauces.

Reduce To fast-boil stock or other liquid in an uncovered pan to evaporate water and concentrate the flavour.

Refresh To cool hot vegetables very quickly by plunging into ice-cold water or holding under cold running water in order to stop the cooking process and preserve the colour.

Roast To cook food by dry heat in the oven.

Roux A mixture of equal quantities of butter (or other fat) and flour cooked together to form the basis of many sauces.

Rubbing in Method of incorporating fat into flour by rubbing between the fingertips, used when a short texture is required. Used for pastry, cakes, scones and biscuits.

Salsa Piquant sauce made from chopped fresh vegetables and sometimes fruit.

Sauté To cook food in a small quantity of fat over a high heat, shaking the pan constantly – usually in a sauté pan (a frying pan with straight sides and a wide base).

Scald To pour boiling water over food to clean it, or loosen skin, eg tomatoes. Also used to describe heating milk to just below boiling point.

Score To cut parallel lines in the surface of food, such as fish (or the fat layer on meat), to improve its appearance or help it cook more quickly.

Sear To brown meat quickly in a little hot fat before grilling or roasting.

Seasoned flour Flour mixed with a little salt and pepper, used for dusting meat, fish etc., before frying.

Shred To grate cheese or slice vegetables into very fine pieces or strips.

Sieve To press food through a perforated sieve to obtain a smooth texture.

Sift To shake dry ingredients through a sieve to remove lumps.

Simmer To keep a liquid just below boiling point.

Skim To remove froth, scum or fat from the surface of stock, gravy, stews, jam etc. Use either a skimmer, a spoon or kitchen paper.

Steam To cook food in steam, usually in a steamer over rapidly boiling water.

Steep To immerse food in warm or cold liquid to soften it, and sometimes to draw out strong flavours.

Stew To cook food, such as tougher cuts of meat, in flavoured liquid which is kept at simmering point.

Stir-fry To cook small even-sized pieces of food rapidly in a little fat, tossing constantly over a high heat.

Sweat To cook chopped or sliced vegetables in a little fat without liquid in a covered pan over a low heat to soften.

Tepid The term used to describe temperature at approximately blood heat, ie 37°C (98.7°F).

Vanilla sugar Sugar in which a vanilla pod has been stored to impart its flavour.

Whipping (whisking) Beating air rapidly into a mixture either with a manual or electric whisk. Whipping usually refers to cream.

Zest The thin coloured outer layer of citrus fruit, which can be removed in fine strips with a zester.

Index